Hiding In Plain Sight

Bringing Our Jewish Family's
Truth to Light

Orlene Allen Gallops

Hiding in Plain Sight

Bringing our Jewish Family's Truth to Light

by Orlene Allen Gallops

First printing, March 2021

Copyright 2021 by Orlene Allen Gallops

ISBN:978-1-7343689-2-5

Editing, design, printing and binding by Two Ems Press

Cover by Scott Baldwin

Post Road Press and Two Ems Press are trade names of Two Ems, Inc.

Two Ems, Inc. 32B Wall Street, Madison CT 06443

203-245-8211   www.two-ems.com

Printed in the United States of America

Front Cover:

L. Larry Allen, M.D. and Eleonore Brahm Allen, parents of the author

Back Cover:

A collage of family members known, or discovered, by the author's search.
He told us very little. Dad, shown upper right in his British Army uniform, spoke to
my sister Susie and me (lower left) in happy terms about his childhood and his parents.
He did tell us that he escaped and joined the British Army in 1939. He also said that
he could never return to Czechoslovakia. The collage pictures family members to Dad's
left and below him. His wife, Eleonore, upper left, his father Jacob Adler, top center, his
mother Julia, below him, and centered, his sister Blanche, with her husband Zoltan Do-
nath. She was a widow when she came to the United States after the war. Blanche was
the only relative we had met, until her sister Kamila visited America in 1961. Lower
center photo shows Orlene Allen Gallops, author of "Hiding In Plain Sight."

Forewords

This is far more than a story. This is a journey of discovery which includes some of the most painful parts of our collective history that unknowingly became part of Orlene's personal past and present. I was overwhelmed by her findings and the bravery to keep going and find so many answers. I was also overwhelmed by the frustration at having so many more questions and dead ends.

Orlene has taken us on her brave journey, an emotional, heartbreaking and joyful mystery and discovery, questioning the foundation of our lives, faith and family. Her story is mesmerizing and moving.

Laura B. Downes, MBA, MLS
   Boston University-Certificate in Genealogy Research

Challenging both the heart and mind, Orlene Allen Gallops balances intimacy with hard core detective work in this book, uncovering a curious family secret that unravels into her family's connection to a universally horrific chapter of history. She invites the reader to take this journey with her and shares an exquisite and deeply personal letter to her parents that underscores this remarkable story of resilience, protection and gifts along the way.

Douglas Eichar, Ph.D.
   Professor Emeritus Sociology, University of Hartford

Embarking

THIS IS a story of uncovering secrets.

I started writing as a way to document four years of intense research about my family. What began as a collection of research results, documents, and discoveries took a path I never could have imagined. The story is complicated and the discoveries were painful and unexpected.

This story is like going on a long-awaited journey with no roadmap. The only direction comes from a ticket stub that you find by chance; it tells you where you got on the highway but has no destination. The trip takes you over miles and miles of roads that turn in every direction, some of which are dead ends. So, you turn around and look for another road. Each time you turn, you are taken along another route which is just as unfamiliar as the one you were just on. You keep searching for a destination but you have none. There are no mile markers, clever billboards or navigation tools to tell you where you are. So, you keep driving and turning, looking for a truth you know is out there.

Your hunger and thirst keep you on the road, looking for an oasis. When you stumble across a sweet, ripe morsel, it's not enough. You want more and more of the same. Sometimes the morsel leaves a bitter aftertaste. Dry crumbly ones make your heart sink with despair, thinking that this is all you will find.

And yet you keep going.

The discovery of having Jewish parents was only one revelation; their families' fate was another. The research documentation was meant to provide my family with the full picture of their Jewish grandparents, great-grandparents and other family members who were survivors or victims of the Holocaust.

Each discovery came with a rush and a high and what came to be a familiar pounding of my heart. Waves of grief would wash over me as I discovered the fate of my family during the Holocaust. I felt compelled to push forward, asking questions in a way I had never done before, looking for the tiniest clue that might lead me somewhere. Mine was a relentless search for answers. What really happened to my family was what I wanted to know.

In the early writing, I had a distinctly clinical approach; I would report the facts and observations. It reminded me of notes I wrote in graduate school about counseling clients; reporting clinical progress and noting observations and recommendations.

But something was missing; I was telling their story based on research and documented facts from their past. It read like a book report and revealed little of their character, their personalities, or our family life. I never said who they really were.

After four years of research and looking at every document and picture over and over again, this story still felt surreal. In contrast to the heart-pounding reaction to each new research finding, I also felt profound sadness and the overwhelming desire to pursue every detail, no matter how small. How quickly I learned that these feelings don't always live in harmony with one another.

As I wrote, I reached a place where I could think about all that I learned without getting teary. Today we call that, "getting some distance." But the distance was becoming uncomfortable. I knew there was more to be said. I knew that I needed to peel back the protective shield I had wrapped around my own feelings. Behind the shield, the words, feelings, and experiences, was the profound grief and sadness of my family's story.

How much more could I grieve about the fate of so many family members? How much longer could I keep asking the question, "why didn't they tell us about their past?" How much more anger could I feel about the events of the Holocaust and the monstrous mass murder of millions of people?

On a cold, gray winter afternoon, I was sitting in my kitchen writing about my mother's background and her ultimate descent into Alzheimer's. It brought me back to the experience of my sister and me coaching her during her last hours. It evoked the vision of our dad beckoning her to join him in peace. It was the first time I ever wrote about witnessing the process of death; the experience was the first time I acknowledged that there is a presence beyond our earthly physical beings.

As I wrote, it became clearer to me that describing my mother's death also led me to be better able to describe her life through my own eyes. This brought me to a place where writing about despair and joy could co-exist. I had been so focused on despair that I lost sight of describing profound happiness, and that is a predominant force in my day-to-day life. Each morning before I get out of bed, I ask myself, "what are the three things that give you joy right this minute?" Each day the answers are a little different although there are predominant themes. Some of these are my husband, my grandchildren, my family, and my dearest friends. Some are rainy Saturdays when John and I have no plans and bask in the early morning tendrils of sleep. I am grateful for my life. Which is maybe the reason confronting so much secret tragedy was even more painful.

I am hopeful that this book will be a source of education and inspiration to others who may embark on family research. It may help them to understand the relentless search for answers and may unlock the history and story of their own families.

This broader and more sweeping vision is to tell this story with optimism. I hope that we will never again witness the atrocities of the Holocaust. I hope we never again tolerate attitudes and behaviors that parallel the thinking and divisiveness that fueled the shattering termination of seven million people.

GRATITUDE

This book is written for all the children, grandchildren, and relatives of those who perished in the Holocaust.

This is the story of one family with a particular secret. They kept it from me and my sister for our entire lives and took it with them when they died.

I also write for my heart; to understand my family, their secrets and motivation behind their shared desire to leave the past behind. I write to better comprehend the energy it takes to keep dark and catastrophic secrets. I also write to celebrate the joy of understanding people who survived the destruction of the Holocaust and found happiness and love.

I write to keep this story alive and remembered so that secrets can no longer be buried; so that we can live in a world where who you are is known and cherished.

I dedicate this book to my grandchildren, Camille Weyland Smith, Claire Margriet Smith, and Weyland Daniel Smith, as descendants of Holocaust victims. They are the loves of my life.

This book would not be possible without the support from my husband John Gallops. John encouraged me to start the research about five years ago and never gave up when I was frustrated, tearful, or hitting a wall in the research process. John gently insisted that we go to Topoľčany, Slovakia in 2016. He cheered me on when I went to Vancouver with my sister to meet one of the only living people who knew my Aunt Blanche. He sat for hours in the National Archives in London with me. He accompanied me to a tearful and difficult meeting with researchers from the Holocaust Museum in Washington, D.C.

John listens, provides feedback, understands my angst, arranges travel plans to explore research possibilities, and never stops being my best friend and husband.

When John and I were married in 2011, he had no idea that we would take this path together. And he would tell you that he never imagined spending his 69th birthday in Topoľčany, Slovakia.

I write for others who contemplate embarking on the journey of family research. Difficult, painful, and sometimes overwhelming, secrets were exposed. They had been held for decades by parents who wished to obliterate their past after experiencing the ravages of the Holocaust. The catastrophic losses, the fear of discovery and persecution, and the desire to protect a family, surely may have been the key motivators to keeping the secrets locked up. I cannot speak for my parents but can say with great certainty that their love for each other and their children shines through their experience like a blanket of hope and determination.

I also write this book with heartfelt gratitude to the many people who encouraged me to continue my research and write about my experience:

My daughter, Bonnie Weyland Smith, listens patiently to my findings and began a spiritual exploration of where she fits into the world of Christianity and Judaism.

My sister, Susan Julia Pitcher, was willing to go to Vancouver, British Columbia with me to meet a woman I found in my research (Judith Gurfinkel). She joined an adventure to Queens, New York to meet with a woman who worked with my Aunt Blanche decades ago. Susie also provided important background details from her perspective. She is three years older than I and her memories helped to confirm or solidify some of the research findings.

Judith Gurfinkel is the only living link to some of the history of my family, stepdaughter to my Aunt Blanche, and one of the loveliest women I have met in my journey. Judith is one of the bright spots in this endeavor.

Carol Lee Harris, mother of my dear friend Claire. Carol encouraged me to start reading about the experiences of children in the Holocaust. She has provided countless books and articles on this topic.

Researchers at the United States Holocaust Memorial Museum in Washington, D.C. whose commitment to preserving the history of the Holocaust and the tireless efforts of their research staff on my behalf. They are treasures of information and compassion.

Two beautiful women in Topoľčany Slovakia who, despite the language barrier, were willing to help me understand what happened to my paternal grandparents.

A lovely and understanding woman from a funeral home in Queens, New York who took the time to research their archives and confirm that my maternal step-grandmother Irma Servos was buried in the Mt. Hebron cemetery. Her willingness to send a letter on my behalf to the executor of Irma Servos' estate is another example of the kindness of so many people I encountered in my research. Through her letter, we were hoping to identify any possible relatives who may have known more about Irma and my mother.

Countless others who took my phone calls, answered my e-mails, and were willing to help me uncover the details of my family history:

Funeral directors in Queens, New York and Topoľčany, Slovakia

Departments of vital statistics in Florida and New York

Staff at the National Archives in London and Army Personnel Center in Glasgow

Researchers from the Mémorial de la Shoah in Paris

Researchers at the University of Bratislava

Staff at the Consulate General of the Slovak Republic

Administrative staff from the City of Cologne, Germany

My sister's friend Ilse Reynolds who helped to translate some of the documents we discovered

A woman from a print shop here in Old Saybrook who understood my anxiety about leaving original documents and pictures overnight in the shop and graciously did the job within a few hours.

And so many others whose paths I crossed in my journey.

A special note to Esther Cohen, the Book Doctor, who has worked as my editor. Esther is more the muse than editor; she challenges me to think about my experience from different perspectives and write descriptively about them. I came to the point in writing when I would ask myself, "What would Esther say about that?" And the output was astonishing to me.

Table of Contents

Beginning the Journey

L. LARRY ALLEN, M.D.
DECEMBER 3, 1914–JULY 29, 1989

◇

ELEONORE BRAHM
APRIL 15, 1929–OCTOBER 30, 1994

THE journey starts in 1994 and takes on a life of its own with a copy of a marriage certificate issued to my parents, Dr. Larry Allen and Eleanore Brahm, in 1949. The ceremony was performed on Henry Street in Lower Manhattan.

At that time, Mom was dying of early onset Alzheimer's disease. In the absence of a birth certificate required by the nursing care facility, I wrote to the New York City Department of Vital Records to request the marriage certificate, which would provide proof of Mom's date of birth.

When I received the document a few weeks later, my eye was quickly drawn to the bottom right-hand section of the certificate which was signed by Rabbi Zeidel Epstein. I kept looking at the signature in a state of disbelief. But at some level, I understood that this was truth for Mom and Dad.

How could this be?

Mom and Dad raised us in the Presbyterian Church. My sister and I were baptized in the Chevy Chase Presbyterian Church outside of the District of Columbia. We were each married by that same Presbyterian minister in the 1970s.

There was never a mention of Jewish heritage.

NEW YORK STATE DEPARTMENT OF ...
Division of Vital Statistics

MARRIAGE LICENSE Registered **M 14947**

...by this Certificate, that any person authorized by law to perform marriage ceremonies within ...to whom this may come, he, not knowing any lawful impediment thereto, is hereby authorized and empowered ...of matrimony between

LARRY LESLIE ALLEN (LEG. CHANGED 1944)

MANHATTAN in the county of ... **NYC** and State of New York

ELEONORE BRAHM ... **FOREST HILLS, L.I.**

...and State of New York and to certify the same to be said parties or either of them under ...seal in his ministerial or official capacity and thereupon he is required to return the certificate in the form herein ...the statements embraced herein or annexed hereto by any subscribed, compile a full and true abstract of all of the facts ...such parties disclosed by their affidavit or verified statements presented to me upon the application for this license.

...application was accompanied by papers complying with the applicable requirements of section thirteen of the ...Relationship Law ... ...by order of a judge or justice.

Testimony Whereof I have hereunto set my hand and affixed the seal of said City at the Municipal Building, Manhattan.

JUN 8 2 25 PM '44   **NOT VALID FOR 24 HOURS**

Shirray W. Stuall
City Clerk

[SEAL]

The following is a full and true abstract of all the facts disclosed by the above-named applicants in their verified statements pre... as me upon their applications for the above license:

FROM THE GROOM:	FROM THE BRIDE:
Full name LARRY LESLIE ALLEN	Full name ELEONORE BRAHM
Color W	Color W
Place of residence 70 E. 96 St.	Place of residence 69-39 Wells 350th Rd.
NYC	Flushing
Date of Birth 11 Dec. 3, 1911	Age B.B. EO April 17, 19..
Occupation PHYSICIAN	Occupation SECRETARY
Place of birth GREECE	Place of birth GERMANY
Full name of father YAKUB ADLER	Full name of father OSCAR BRAHM
Country of birth of father GREECE	Country of birth of father GERMANY
Full maiden name of mother JULIA SCHLESINGER	Full maiden name of mother IRMA SERVOS
Country of birth of mother GREECE	Country of birth of mother GERMANY
How many times have you been married NONE	How many times have you been married NONE
Full names of husbands during former marriages	Full names of husbands during former marriages
Are they living or dead	Are they living or dead
Are you a divorced person	Are you a divorced person
When and where and against whom was divorce or an... or dissolution granted	
Where did you live last	

Jere Epstein ... Ma ... ... Roth ...
residing at _170 Henry St. N.Y. ... N.Y._

a _minister_ ... State of New York, do hereby certify that I did on this
First day of _July_ in the year A.D. 1944 at _Bronx 173 Henry_
_St._ in the county of ... and State of New York, solemnize the Rite of Matrimony between

Harry Leslie Allen
of _70 E 96th_ in the county of _Manhattan_ and State of New York and
Eleanore Brahm
of _69-39 Woodside_ in the county of _Forest Hills_ and State of New York in the
presence of _Celia H. Rosengarten_ _Lee Miller_
who were and are named thereto in letters annexed.

Witness my hand at _173 Henry St._ in the county of _N.Y._
...

In presence of _Celia H. Rosengarten_   _Ruth Epstein Daleh_
500 Grand Street

Lee Miller   _173 Henry St. N.Y._
49-39 Flushing Blvd 6/309
Forest Hills 23, N.Y.

My Family

MY SISTER Susan (within our family, she is known as Susie) is three years older than I. Mom used to call her "Susie-belle" and me "Orlenie-belle."

Many people think Susie and I look exactly alike, though we don't see the resemblance to each other. She is a tall, olive-skinned, dark-haired woman who exudes a sense of style and what I would call "flash." She has beautiful brown eyes and the long legs of a dancer. When she speaks, her hands don't stop moving. She dresses in bright vibrant colors regardless of fashion trends. I think she is a woman who knows her own style.

By contrast, I am a few inches shorter than my sister and am fairer-skinned with bluish-green eyes. I have the same dark hair as Susie, although I wear mine much shorter. I too speak with my hands, especially when I'm excited about something. Although Susie and I may look alike, we are completely different women, which adds dimension to our relationship.

The author and her sister, Washington, D.C., circa 1960

Susie has been happily married to her husband Bill for 46 years. She had a stellar career in buying and merchandising and, later on, joined her husband's law firm as the Operations Director. She has two children: my nephew Paul who lives in Toronto and my niece Julia who lives close to Annapolis. Julia has two beautiful children: Colt, who is five years old and Oliver, who turned three last year.

Like my sister, I have experienced the joy of having grandchildren. My daughter Bonnie and her husband Luke have three children: Camille, who is thirteen, Claire, who is eleven, and Weyland, who is eight.

The author with husband John (2011)
Photo Credit: Leslie Dumke Studio

I married my second husband in 2011 and am loving a relationship that is completely right for me. John has taken on "my crew" and treats them like his own. He comes from a very close-knit family, most of whom live in Georgia and Tennessee. His brother and his wife live in Lyon, France. John's entire family has taken me in as their own as well, so I'm a fortunate woman to have married into an extended family.

My husband John is not a "pretty boy," which is what attracts me to him. His face is one of a man who has spent a lot of time outdoors; worn in just the right places, with evidence of having spent time in the sun. His green eyes, framed by tortoise shell glasses, light up when he smiles and stare intently at whatever he happens to be doing. He always looks focused. Like so many men his age, his hair is soft gray and cut in a buzzed style, which gives him a rather distinguished look.

He wears jeans, a turtleneck shirt, and fleece-lined hooded sweatshirt all winter, which suits his laid-back style. When he walks, it is with a slow, methodical pace, which is how he approaches everything he does, as though he is never in a frantic rush to get anywhere. He stands about 5'10" with broad shoulders and shapely legs. He speaks with a soft southern drawl, which is part of his charm. When he is content, I can hear him humming softly; not a particular tune, but just humming. This is a man who mows the backyard when the grandchildren come so their feet won't be itchy from the grass when they play outside.

◇ GROWING UP ◇

Our tight-knit family of four was nearly the only one my sister and I knew. We knew one of our aunts through our early childhood, Dad's sister Blanche who lived in the Bronx, New York. We knew another sister Kamila lived in Czechoslovakia; we met her once when she visited the U.S. But we had no grandparents, cousins, or uncles.

We were raised in a traditional way with the European influence of Dad, from Czechoslovakia, and Mom, from France. Both were naturalized U.S. citizens with love and passion for their adopted country. They met in Paris on Bastille Day in 1946 and came to the U.S. separately, but married in New York in 1949.

Mom spoke so lovingly of Dad's marriage proposal. He presented her with a diamond ring that he had carried with him through the war; the story is that it belonged to his family. They stayed in love throughout their 40-year marriage, anyone could see it.

They were each other's worlds and Susie and I were the loving outcome of their marriage. Mom used to say that Susie was a "blessing in disguise."

We were to find out later what that really meant.

The author's parents, Baltimore, Maryland - Easter 1968

What a beautiful couple they made.

Mom was a petite, fair-skinned, dark haired, green-eyed woman who spoke beautiful English with a hint of a French accent. She used to tell us that she learned to speak English by going to English-only movies. She had a smile that lit up her entire face and she possessed a lively temperament. Mom had what I would describe as an uncanny "sixth sense" or intuition. She could easily assess a situation or a person. She could read between the lines or predict an outcome like no one else I've ever known.

An incredibly sexy woman, she had a beautiful body and was remarkably tuned in to her own sexuality. She made no secret of the fact that she and my dad were active lovers. And when it came time to talk to me about sex and love, she didn't hold back. There was no question that went unanswered.

In contrast to Mom's fair complexion, Dad was olive-skinned with dark hair and brown eyes. He was built on the stocky side and had a brisk and purposeful gait when he walked. Just like Mom, he had a wonderful smile. His English, although excellent, was not as proficient as Mom's and he spoke with a heavy Czech accent.

◊

I often wonder how he was able to learn English after he left Czechoslovakia in 1939 to join the British Army.

◊

He was an excitable man by temperament who spoke rapidly and gestured with his arms and hands if he was angered about something, particularly if it involved perceived harm to anyone he loved or violated a principle he believed in. He was highly principled in his thoughts and actions and had little patience for anything or anyone who didn't display the same sentiments. He spoke with few filters, so you always knew where you stood. He placed high value on education and was a bit of an intellectual "snob." I don't mean this in a negative way; he was never condescending or patronizing to people who weren't at his level, but at the same time, made it clear that being intelligent and formally well-educated were the keys to independence. In his more traditional thinking, a woman needed education, should she remain single or become widowed or divorced.

◊

In my opinion, education is not a contingency plan based on marital status. Understanding the generational differences, I don't fault him and am grateful to have had the educational opportunities he provided.

◊

His view of education withstood the test of time. My career choices and possibilities would have been severely limited without advanced education. I took this thinking to heart as I raised my daughter. Her education was the best gift I could provide to enable her independence and ability to pursue the work she loves.

◊

Dad had a deep and infectious laugh that lit up his whole face and made his eyes twinkle. He had a wonderful sense of humor. He used to say, "Mom and I wanted to marry on July 4, but the courts were closed for the national holiday and that was the day I lost my independence." He was the most independent man you could ever meet!

◊

I believed and loved this story until I saw the marriage certificate. That was the day it fell apart. But I still laugh when I think of him telling the story.

◊

Mom and Dad's loyalty to us, as their children, was ferocious. They held us tight to their hearts and souls. Sometimes it felt suffocating, like a veil around us that was impenetrable to the outside.

They were a highly social couple in their earlier years, developing friendships and close relationships, but were very closed about any discussion of family matters outside our nucleus.

◊

It is only much later on that this dynamic became understandable to me and my sister.

◊

Mom and Dad were masters at keeping secrets.

◊

I understand now that this characteristic carries out generationally in ways that we can't even imagine. And what a relief to know that secrets can be known. I understand so much better now that feelings of shame, embarrassment, and lack of control are often the drivers of secret-keeping. For my parents, I can only postulate (and empathize) that their secrets were kept out of fear of persecution and a desire to protect their family by erasing their catastrophic experiences.

◊

As we were growing up, we moved around frequently. Dad had a post in a hospital in Buffalo, New York until we moved to Patchogue, Long Island in about 1955 where he opened a private radiology practice. He and Mom worked long hours, seven days a week. They also built a house on Roe Avenue in the process.

We had a lovely life there. We lived in a beautiful little home with loving and caring parents who completely adored us. Although I was only about four years old at the time, I remember Dad bringing chocolate ice cream home any time my sister or I were sick. There was a wonderfully comforting way about him. I remember falling down in the front yard, tearing open my left hand on the corner of a slate walkway, and needing stitches in my right hand. As much as it hurt, I was more disappointed about that fall because it meant we couldn't go to a local carnival that night. Dad made the time entertaining and fun, even though his decision was that I needed to be home with my injured hand.

The year that my sister and I had our tonsils removed was memorable. I was five and Susie was eight. We went at the same time and came home to find brand new "Tiny Tears" dolls awaiting. I still have that doll, although her curled hair has been permanently altered by my earlier childhood attempts to wash, style, and cut it. My sister's doll looks as new as it did the day she received it.

It was also the time that Dad probably saved Susie's life. She started bleeding from the tonsillectomy. I could only hear her sounds, as our rooms were separated by a double-louvered door. I remember hearing Dad's swift actions as he came through the doors to respond and offer his comforting voice to a frightened eight-year-old.

As I think back, their caring and fussing over us imbedded something permanent. Throughout our lives, we were treated like royalty in the rare times that we were sick. I am a living embodiment to this, with my daughter when she was still living at home, and now to my husband, who actually prefers less fussing if he is ill.

My sister ministers care in the same way. I remember her staying up all night with me when we were together in Rehoboth Beach, Delaware many summers ago. I was violently sick for hours and she never left my side. She cares for her husband and family in the same way.

What I learned from this is that everyone needs mothering when they don't feel well. I still need it when I'm sick: the fussing and caring make me feel loved, and experiencing that love is precious motivation to get better. I can't ever remember faking illness as so many children do, although Mom would have caught on in an instant and it's hard to feign illness when your dad is a doctor. How many times have I told my daughter, "No one takes better care of you when you are sick than your mother." We always have a great laugh about that as if we understand instinctively what it means to be nurtured and to nurture. I don't think my mom had this kind of love in her experience and I am still astounded at her ability to nurture in this way.

Within a few short years of living in Patchogue, Mom and Dad decided that the small-town environment wasn't working for them. They later talked about the bias they felt as foreigners, particularly as they both spoke with accents. It would never have occurred to me, as I was growing up, that an accent was something to fear or use as a way to reject another individual.

In the late 1950s, we moved to Washington, D.C. to an apartment on Connecticut Avenue. I started first grade and Susie entered fourth. Dad had a new role with the Veterans Administration Central Office. He made that decision based on his need to give back to his adopted country, to serve those in need, and also to be able to spend more time with his family; his "girls" as he called us.

The city life was very appealing to them, but in 1961 we moved to Arlington, Virginia. We lived in a beautiful high-rise apartment building on Columbia Turnpike that overlooked the Arlington National Cemetery.

During the summer of 1962, we took a road trip to California for a vacation. Susie and I didn't know that Dad was talking to one of the V.A. hospitals in Southern California about a possible move. The car he bought for this trip, a Rambler station wagon, was outfitted with white and red dotted-swiss curtains on the side windows that were fashioned by our Aunt Blanche. This was before seat belt regulations took effect, so Susie and I stretched out in the back of the wagon, played games, fought with each other and otherwise were entertained throughout this adventure. Unfortunately, the Rambler didn't make it further than Flagstaff, Arizona where we spent a few days waiting for repairs after it overheated on a desert highway.

When we returned to Virginia, the next thing we knew was that we were moving West. This time in a 1962 Cadillac; Dad wasn't taking any more chances. Off we went. Two years later, we took yet another road trip to the East Coast for the World's Fair in Queens. What a trip that was! We also were able to spend time with Dad's sister, Blanche.

We stayed in California for about four years and lived in a beautiful house in Northridge; Dad had a pool put in and we spent hours swimming and enjoying our lovely surroundings. I have memories of cookouts on the patio when he got home from work, trips to some of the wonderful California attractions (Disneyland, San Francisco, the Muir Forest), and countless other excursions.

One infamous trip to Tijuana, Mexico, with a camper attached to the car, was cut short as a result of riots in the Watts area of Los Angeles. We returned home sooner than planned. Dad was worried about the potential harm that could come to us, just by being in the wrong place at the wrong time.

He was quite adventurous and made it a point to show us the places and things that are the fabric of our country. I've counted six cross-country car trips we took between 1962 and 1966, each one with a different driving route. To this day, when I speak to a colleague from another part of the country I have lived in, or seen on a trip, I can remember being there. It's a great gift for establishing professional rapport; probably not what Dad had in mind, but it works. His perspective was to embrace new horizons and never look back.

◊

This philosophy became clearer to me much later in my discoveries of my family.

◊

In 1966, we made another move, back to the East Coast, to live in Baltimore, Maryland. Dad had a new position there as Chief Radiologist at the Veterans Hospital at the corner of Loch Raven Boulevard and the Alameda. His long-term goal was to get back to New York City, where he and Mom had started their new life in the U.S. Dad, being who he was, achieved that goal.

In 1968, we moved to Forest Hills, New York where he took a post at the Outpatient V.A. Clinic on Ryerson Street in Brooklyn as the Chief Radiologist. Susie was going off to college in Delaware that fall, and I was starting my sophomore year at

raised her. Her memories of her were haunting; she spoke about being locked in closets and abused by this woman. We were to find out much later that Mom didn't know Irma was her stepmother until around the time my sister was born. All those years she believed Irma was her biological mother.

◇

Photo of Blanche, discovered in her apartment after her death (date unknown)

Mom spoke of the bombings in Paris during World War II and how the sound of the silence and the shrill screams of the sirens never really left her. She spoke so affectionately of her father, saying that she looked for his face in crowds, hoping to find him again. She spoke of her intense feeling about the Germans and their harsh and inhumane treatment of people during the war.

Dad used to say he would never buy a German car or product; both of them refused to go back to Europe for any reason.

My sister and I remember Mom and Dad offering us the opportunity to go to Europe, Susie to attend school in Switzerland and me to spend a semester abroad when I was in college. This was such a contradiction to their own reluctance or refusal to go back to Europe.

In my case, they offered the semester abroad as a way to convince me to live the dormitory life in college. At that time, my decision was to commute to undergraduate school from home and get married to my boyfriend. I think they were hoping I would expand my world experience and possibly delay getting married, but they went along with my decision.

Their true love was their new country here in the U.S. My parents loved and adored what they called their "adopted country." Dad used to say that this was the only country where you could criticize the government or powers that be and not get shot or jailed.

Mom also spoke of living with the nuns during the war.

◊

I never really understood the meaning of that until much later.

◊

She also lived with a family in Switzerland and stayed in touch with them after she came to the U.S. Maybe this is why they offered Switzerland as a place for my sister to study.

Mom lived with a terrible fear of being abandoned by those she loved. She and my dad were each other's worlds as far back as I can remember. You never knew a more devoted couple who had such love in their hearts, for each other and for their children. Protective, generous, loving, sometimes controlling and authoritative, they put our little family first above everything else.

To watch my mother's face light up when she saw my dad walking in the door at the end of the day was like watching magic. And to see him smile and walk a little faster to greet us was indescribable. I still see that face when I think of him.

◊

We lost this dear man on July 29, 1989 as a result of a massive cerebral hemorrhage and thankfully, he died peacefully with no pain. And how sad I felt when three months later, the Berlin Wall came down. How my Dad would have celebrated that!

◊

Questions Without Answers

◇ CZECH FAMILIES DON'T HAVE NAMES
LIKE ALLEN ◇

AT SOME point in time, when my sister and I were older, we began to question mom and dad about our family history. Always, always, always, we were met with evasive answers or gross generalities.

We asked about our family name, Allen. How could this be our name if Dad was born in Czechoslovakia? Czechs don't have names like that. He would never answer the question.

My sister once asked him directly, and I think quite bravely, if he was Jewish and he replied, "Are you kidding? Don't be silly."

If we questioned Mom about her years during World War II, she would say, "it's best to let sleeping dogs lie." Dad used to say we should look forward, not look back.

◇

I only understand now what that really meant to him.

◇

There were other inklings that stirred the wondering. Some of the major philosophical statements and ideologies that Mom and Dad held were confusing and disjointed to me, both as a child, and later as a young adult. Although they were raising us in traditional Christian values, they were adamant that Jesus was not the son of God; that he was a great prophet and we should live by his teachings. We didn't have a lot of discussion about it, but their thoughts were perfectly clear.

At the same time, both of them wore beautiful gold crosses, as did my sister and I. Susie and I were both married in a Presbyterian Church in Queens, New York by the same Presbyterian minister who baptized us and who officiated at our parents' second marriage ceremony in the early 1960s.

All of the traditional Christian holidays, celebrated with wonderful food cooked by Mom, were often shared with friends who came for the occasion. Our parents were wonderful hosts and loved to entertain in the earlier years, yet Mom still told us not to drink milk with a salami sandwich.

Dad's Escape from Czechoslovakia and Enlistment in the British Army

DAD ENLISTED in the British Army, Auxiliary Military Pioneer Corps, embodied territorial Army in 1939 when he graduated from medical school in Bratislava. When he left or escaped from Czechoslovakia, his name was Ladislav Adler. In 1941, he was transferred to the Royal Army Medical Corps and released in 1942 to attend University of Glasgow Medical School.

I wish I knew how he was able to learn the English language

The author's father in military dress (British Army) 1944

so quickly, coming from Eastern Europe. With bias, I can tell you that he was bright, resourceful, and always looking for the opportunity to learn new things. I also think his situation demanded a rapid assimilation into the English language. His English was excellent, though not always grammatically perfect, and he spoke with a heavy Czech accent.

He rejoined in 1943 and was appointed to an Emergency Commission as Lieutenant with the Royal Army Medical Corps and the following year was promoted to War Substantive Captain. In 1944, he changed his name from Ladislav Adler to Leslie Allen.

In 1946, he relinquished his commission and was granted honorary rank of Captain. He lived in England in Stamford Hill until 1948 and became a United Kingdom citizen during that time. Stamford Hill is an area of Inner London, located about five miles northeast of Charing Cross. The neighborhood is a sub-district of Hackney, the major component of the London Borough of Hackney, and is known for its Jewish Hasidic community.

He emigrated to New York City, U.S., from Southampton, England in February of 1948. Dad lived on the Upper West Side in Manhattan and, as I understand it, was reunited with Mom when he arrived in the United States. They met at a party in Paris on Bastille Day in 1946 and came to the U.S. separately. I don't know the circumstances around their reunion but they married in 1949.

Dad's military history is well documented. Unknown to us, he kept these records in his safe, discovered by my sister and me after his death. I also spent time at the National Archives in London in 2017 where records of his service were available.

Prior to going to London, I wanted to find out if there was any information that could lead me to understand how he got out of Czechoslovakia in 1939. I sent formal requests to the Army Personnel Centre in Glasgow, Scotland as well as the National Archives in London. Although neither institution could answer questions about his departure from Czechoslovakia, the staff researchers at the National Archives were immensely helpful in pointing me to where we would find his records.

Of particular note was the response from the Army Personnel Centre in Glasgow. They provided his full military file which includes correspondence during his service as well as documents surrounding his name change. I remember the package I received from my contact. He sent me the original Army Book 64 "Soldier's Service and Pay Book" that belonged to my dad. It contained information on his leave from the Army, pay records, medical classification, vaccination and in-

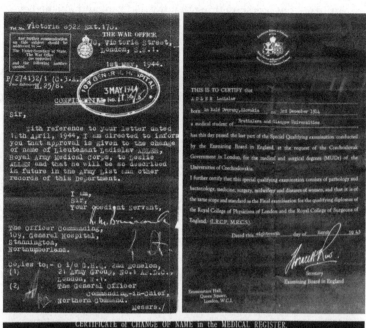

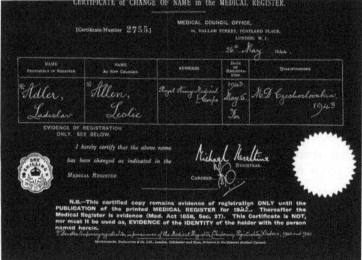

Records of Leslie Allen's name change in 1944, discovered in his safe after his death

oculation records, and his clothing sizes. Nothing out of the ordinary, but it is something that my dad kept and touched every day he served in the Army, complete with the ink stains on the inside pages.

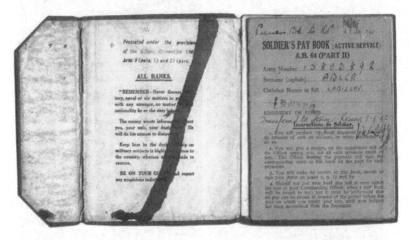

Soldier's Pay Book cover (courtesy of the Glasgow Personnel Centre)

This was yet another testament to the kindness and willingness of people completely unknown to me who took the extra step and made the effort to help. I continue to be awed and inspired by the people I have made contact with throughout this research journey.

After he came to the United States in 1948, Dad went through a long and arduous process to obtain licensure to practice medicine here.

In June 1951, he wrote to the Secretary-Treasurer of the American Board of Radiology in Rochester, Minnesota to request an application to apply for the Roentgenological Board Examinations. At the time, he was finishing his second year at Bellevue Hospital in New York and was preparing to start his third year at the Francis Delafield Hospital (affiliated with the Columbia Medical Center).

Having been told that he was not eligible to sit for the Boards because of his citizenship status (at the time he was a United Kingdom citizen), he wrote to ask if he could sit for the exam with the provision that the certification be withheld until his citizenship was completed.

In June of 1952, he received a letter that the Board of Trustees of the American Board of Radiology had agreed to this request. He successfully passed the Boards in December of 1952 and in June of 1953 was able to present his certificate of Naturalization to the Radiology Board.

This glimpse of my dad's persistence to pursue his dream, and hope for his future here in the U.S., is only one shining example of the qualities that carried him through this arduous process and throughout his life.

RL

" 1 FEB 1947

N.10.e.
Any communication on the subject
of this letter should be addressed to:-
THE UNDER SECRETARY OF STATE,
HOME OFFICE,
and the following number quoted:

Nationality Division,
Home Office,
Whitehall,
London, S.W.1

A.13559/3/Nat.Div.

31st January, 1947.

Your Ref: VF.

Gentlemen,

1   I am directed by the Secretary of State to inform you that he is prepared in pursuance of the British Nationality and Status of Aliens Acts, 1914/1933, to grant a Certificate of Naturalization to your client, Mr. L. Allen , on condition that he will give an assurance in writing that he will not take any steps to retain or recover his Czechoslovak nationality and that he will not, if naturalized a British subject, thereafter look for protection from, nor claim allegiance to, the country of which he is at present a national.

2   The Secretary of State thinks it right to add that he must not assume that his naturalization in this country will entitle him or his children (if any) to be regarded by the Czechoslovak authorities as British subjects unless they cease by Czechoslovak law to possess Czechoslovak nationality. Until he has actually ceased to possess Czechoslovak nationality His Majesty's Government will not be able to afford him any assistance or protection in Czechoslovakia as against the Czechoslovak authorities.

On receipt of the assurance asked for, and on payment of the prescribed fee of Ten/Nine Pounds, the Certificate will be forwarded to you as soon as possible.

Fees should be sent by post to the Finance Branch, Home Office, Cornwall House, Stamford Street, S.E.1.   Post Office Orders, Postal Orders or Cheques should be made payable to the Accounting Officer, Home Office, and crossed "Bank of England:
Messrs. Blyth,Dutton,Wright & Bennett,   /Account
    112, Gresham House,
        Old Broad Street,London, E.C.2.

Letter related to Dr. Allen's British citizenship, and requirements for the future.
(discovered in father's safe after his death)

B.R. Kirklin, M.D.   June 10th,1951.
Secretary-Treasurer,
The American Board of
Radiology,
Rochester,Minnesota.

Dear Doctor Kirklin,
                    I would like to apply for the Roentgenological
Board Examinations in June 1952.Would you kindly send me the
necessary application forms.

                    I had one year of X-Ray Diagnosis at Goldwater
Memorial Hospital,July 1949 till June 1950.At present I am finishing
my second year at Bellevue Hospital,Radiation Therapy.

                    In July 1951 I am starting my third year at
Francis Delafield Hospital affiliated with Columbia Medical Center.

                         Thanking you,
                         Yours Sincerely,

                         Leslie Larry Allen,M.D.

Correspondence to the American Board of Radiology 1951-1952

December 5, 1951

Dr. B.R. Kirklin
Secretary
American Board of Radiology
Mayo Clinic
Rochester, Minn.

Dear Doctor Kirklin,

I received your letter of November 26th, 1951, and I regret
that I am not this time eligible for examination.

At present I am a citizen of Great Britain, but I shall be
eligible for my final papers in 8 months after the examination
date.

I wonder if I might suggest for your consideration the possibility
of my taking the examination at this time and you withholding
the certification until such time as my final papers are
completed.

If the above suggestion does not meet with your approval,
then I should appreciate your retaining the examination fee until
the time I am eligible.

Thank you for your kind consideration,

Sincerely yours,

The American Board of Radiology

OFFICE OF THE SECRETARY-TREASURER

B. R. KIRKLIN

MAYO CLINIC

ROCHESTER, MINNESOTA

December 13, 1951

Dr. Leslie Larry Allen
99 Fort Washington Avenue
New York 32, New York

Dear Doctor Allen:

This will acknowledge your letter of December 5.
I regret that I do not have the authority to give you
permission to appear for examination before you have your
final citizenship papers. This can be done only by an
unanimous vote of the Board of Trustees of the American
Board of Radiology. I shall be glad to bring this matter
up before their next meeting in Chicago this coming June
and report to you shortly thereafter.

Sincerely yours,

B. R. Kirklin, M.D.

The American Board of Radiology

OFFICE OF THE SECRETARY-TREASURER

B. R. KIRKLIN

MAYO CLINIC

ROCHESTER, MINNESOTA

June 24, 1952

Dr. Leslie Larry Allen
99 Fort Washington Avenue
New York 32, New York

Dear Doctor Allen:

This is to inform you that at our recent
meeting it was agreed to permit you to appear for
examination at our December meeting in Cincinnati.
If you are not a full citizen of the United States
at that time and if your examination is successful,
your certificate will be withheld until you are
a full citizen and you have submitted proof to this
effect.

You will hear from us early this fall regarding an appointment in December.

Sincerely yours,

B. R. Kirklin, M.D.

BRK:KEG
cc Dr. Ira I. Kaplan

The American Board of Radiology

DEAR DOCTOR:

I am pleased to inform you that at its last meeting The American Board of
Radiology voted to grant you its certificate in RADIOLOGY

With personal congratulations, I am

Sincerely yours,

Secretary

DR. Leslie Larry Allen

Roswell Park Memorial Institute

Buffalo 3, New York

DECEMBER 6TH 1953

Final communication from the American Board of Radiology,
granting board certifcation to practice in the U.S.

Secrets Start Unraveling

◇ BLANCHE APPEARS AT BLOOMINGDALE'S ◇

MANY YEARS later, in 1973, things really began to unravel. I was getting married to my first husband that year and my sister was planning her wedding date for 1974. Our house was full of excitement and wedding drama.

Early in 1973, my mother called me at my fiancé's house and asked me to come home right away. She said it was urgent. Understanding that my mom sometimes overreacted to things, I was still scared. I had no idea what was wrong.

As the story goes, my sister, who was living in Manhattan at the time, had called to say that she ran into Aunt Blanche at Bloomingdale's, where Susie worked as a buyer. Susie related to Mom that Blanche had approached her and wanted to get together, that she had some "stories" to tell her. We don't know if that meeting was coincidence or if Blanche had sought Susie out. When Susie related this to Mom, all hell broke loose.

When I returned home, Mom sat me down in the den off of the kitchen; she was completely unglued. Through her tears, she told me that she was the illegitimate child of a relationship between her father, Oskar Brahm, and his mistress, whose name we now know was Ellen Schwarz. He was married to Irma Servos at the time my mother was born. From what we know, Mom found this out around the time that Susie was born* and the emotional impact was catastrophic for her. Susie was indeed the "blessing in disguise" who kept Mom focused.

◇

* Excerpt from Crofton Convalescent Center, Crofton, Maryland "Resident and Social History" (provided by Nursing Home Staff to Susan Pitcher (author's sister) November 13, 1992:

"...their daughter, Susan, was born in 1950, and it was about this time that Mrs. Allen learned the

truth about her parentage. It was a great shock
and Mrs. Allen had what was later described as a
'nervous breakdown,' but Susan knows no details.
She (Mrs. Allen) always referred to her daughter's
arrival as a 'blessing in disguise'."

Evidently Blanche may have known this, or Mom wouldn't have been so frightened of us finding out. I don't know what else she thought Blanche may have shared with Susie, but the impact was that Mom was terrified. She was teary, apologetic and completely unraveled at this disclosure. Although I was surprised, I asked her why she never told us and her response was, "because I thought you wouldn't love me." I remember telling her that loving her would never change, that this was not her fault and I wished she had not sat on this painful secret for so long. Susie heard the same story, and Mom forbade her from calling Blanche.

That was the last we heard of Blanche. And still Mom never divulged that she was Jewish.

◊

As I look back on this piece of my history, I still wonder
what really happened between Blanche and my mom and dad.
Other research and personal testimony paint
a completely different picture of Blanche as a person.

◊

Their Marriage Certificate

THEIR MARRIAGE certificate surfaced in 1994 at the time Mom was dying of early onset Alzheimer's. Since we couldn't locate a birth record, I sent a letter to the New York City Department of Vital Statistics to request their marriage certificate, which would provide proof of her date of birth.

It was signed by Rabbi Zeidel Epstein. I stared at the Rabbi's signature in disbelief, but somehow this is what we had been waiting for. It was a confirmation of so many questions about Mom and Dad that had flickered throughout our growing up years, but were never brought to light.

Another significant detail on the marriage certificate, was that Mom's birthplace was listed as Germany. We were brought up to believe she had been born in Paris, France. Mom and Dad often spoke French at home and we would never have known that she may have also been fluent in German. Dad spoke multiple languages: French, English, Russian, Polish, and Czech.

We had been told Mom and Dad were married by a Justice of the Peace, never a mention of a Rabbi, or that they were Jewish. We knew that they had taken their vows again in a wedding ceremony in the Chevy Chase Presbyterian Church outside of Washington D.C. when I was about five years old and Susie was eight.

At the time of this discovery, my sister and I were in the midst of caring for Mom, who was in the last stages of life. There wasn't much time or emotional energy to devote to the topic of Mom and Dad's marriage certificate. I think we were both in a state of disbelief; yet we knew this was the answer to the question of our heritage.

Susie was raising her family and caring for her mother-in-law, and I was raising Bonnie, working full-time and finishing graduate school.

After Mom's death in 1994, the presence of that marriage

certificate drove me to start asking more questions. During that time, I shared information from the marriage certificate with friends, in particular my friend Carole Harris who is Jewish. Carole is the mother of my dear friend Claire Harris. As part of a group of old friends who are like family to me, Carole was very interested in knowing my family's Jewish history.

Carole is one of the most elegant looking women I know. Petite with short blondish-brown hair and big brown eyes, she carries herself with grace and poise. She is outspoken in her opinions about all things, from politics to decorating, and has been a wonderful addition to our multi-generational group.

She was also excited and enthusiastic about my Jewish history. I think Carole may have been the first person to tell me that in Jewish law, you are Jewish if your mother is Jewish.

Although it was years before my discoveries came to light, Carole encouraged me to learn and read more about the Holocaust. One of the first books I read was "The Hidden Children" by Jane Marks. Ms. Marks writes a compelling story of coping and survival through the eyes of Holocaust victims. Until I read this book, I had only a high-school level view of the history of the Holocaust without really understanding the cataclysmic impact for millions of people. Carole continued to provide additional books and encouragement for me to find out more about my family.

When I was in graduate school, I read "Man's Search for Meaning" by Viktor Frankl as part of my studies in counseling. Dr. Frankl's internment at Auschwitz was yet another glimpse into the horrors that were experienced by Jews in Europe during World War II. I don't think I really understood this at the time.

Having reread the book over the years and in light of my family's fate, the basis of his writing and his remarkable ability to shift his paradigm and survive, is a testament to what people endure in traumatic circumstances. Dr. Frankl's work is the underpinning of many approaches to counseling. I now use and recommend his book as an example in many group settings that I facilitate in the course of my professional life.

In 1998, the year my daughter started college, I went to visit a Rabbi at Beth El Temple in West Harford, Connecticut. I brought the marriage certificate as well as the few other documents I had from Dad. The Rabbi affirmed everything I thought in terms of their being Jewish. It felt so right to hear someone else state, with conviction, that in 1949 a Rabbi would not have married two people who were not both Jewish. I can't count how many times I said that to myself, yet I still felt a level of disbelief. The disbelief was a complete disconnect to the notion that Mom and Dad would never have lied about anything. To question them felt disloyal.

Copy of marriage certificate (1949)

I shared more documents with the Rabbi; Dad's medical school records and the documentation of his name change in 1944 when he was in the British Army. We found these in his safe after his death. Ladislav Adler became Larry Allen and the past was gone. The Rabbi gently asked what I wanted to do with this information. My answer was, "nothing." The knowledge and expert confirmation that Mom and Dad were Jewish were all I needed to know at the time. I thought I was done with this.

I put this aside for many years. Life was hectic with little time to pursue a major research endeavor, and the web-based and digital records were not as robust as they are today. You might ask, "what was the catalyst to start this research in 2015?"

The answer isn't straight-forward.

At the time, I was looking very seriously at my faith and where I stood with it. I had reached a place of questioning, learning, and doubting. As I grew and opened up to examining my faith, it raised more questions rather than answering. Some of the questions coninued to be about my family, about their secret and wanting to know more about them.

My husband encouraged me to follow the path to research. I kept thinking about the marriage certificate; I looked at it more than once, to remind myself that they were, in fact, married by a Rabbi.

The marriage certificate became the focus of my search for answers. It was one of the few pieces of information I had to go on. I kept thinking about the Rabbi's signature; I kept wondering if he might have records or information that could reveal more.

The author's parents at Susan's wedding, 1974

Starting My Research and Resurrecting the Past

IT WAS years later when the calling came to pursue my family history and see what else I could discover. My husband had been encouraging me to pursue this; what he observed was that the unanswered questions I kept raising were becoming impossible to ignore.

◇

Why didn't Mom and Dad tell us they were Jewish?
Why did they make up the story about
where they were married in 1949?
Why did they wear crosses around their necks?
Why did Dad change his name?
Why did Dad say that Jesus was not the Son of God?
Why do I feel like an imposter when I'm in a church?

◇

I kept putting off the research. I really didn't know where to start. There was no one who could provide any oral history, no other family or friend who might have known. But the calling became intense.

As I look back, I think it was emerging from the conflict I was experiencing in pursuing a late-life faith journey. I couldn't reconcile the messages I was hearing in a church setting with what I had heard in my childhood. As a child and adolescent, when you worship in church with your parents and attend Sunday school, the message is that Jesus is the Son of God, the Savior.

Outside of church, when your parents talk about Jesus being a prophet and visionary, not the Son of God, it creates conflict that cannot be resolved. My response to the conflict was to push all religion aside and define myself as "spiritual."

My Search for Rabbi Epstein

RABBI ZEIDEL Epstein performed my parents' marriage ceremony on July 5, 1949 on Henry Street in lower Manhattan. Perhaps this was the answer for so many questions about Mom and Dad that flickered throughout our childhood but were never answered.

I wanted to know more about Rabbi Epstein with the hope that I could find more information about my parents' wedding ceremony, or any other information that Rabbi Epstein might have. I did a web search, which led me to the Rabbi Joseph Jacob School in Manhattan. This led to an article written by Rabbi Marvin Schick in which he referenced Rabbi Epstein in his commentary. I was compelled to write to Rabbi Schick in the hope that more information would come to light.

Tuesday, February 17, 2015

Good morning, Rabbi Schick. I left a message with your office that I had called to see if you might be able to provide some guidance.

I was so sorry to hear about your brother's death from your staff at the Jacob Joseph School; please accept my sympathy in your loss.

I came across your history in the article in the Jewish Press (http://www.Jewishishpress.com/indepth/front-page/the-rabbi-jacob-joseph-school-and-me/2014/10/29/0/) and was particularly drawn to your reference to Rabbi Zeidel Epstein. While I am not 100% sure, I believe that Rabbi Epstein may have presided over my parents' wedding ceremony in 1949 at the 173 Henry Street location. The marriage certificate I have names him as the presiding clergy at the Henry Street location.

Of interest to me is some of the information on their marriage certificate. As I mentioned, Rabbi Epstein presided over their ceremony (July 5, 1949) at the address of 173 Henry Street, New

York, NY. One of the witnesses of the ceremony was an individual named Miller (the first name is difficult to decipher). This individual may have been my mother's stepmother who accompanied her when she came to the U.S. by boat in 1948. The information on the passenger list (from ancestry. com) lists my mother as well as a woman named Irma Mullerova, who is noted on the document as her mother. My assumption is that Mrs. Mullerova is the same person as the Miller listed on my parent's marriage certificate. Based on the marriage certificate, Mrs. Miller's address at that time was the same as my mother's.

If my logic and information is correct, Mrs. Miller was married to my mother's father until his death in 1943; my recent research fully documents his death at the hands of the Nazis at Auschwitz. Mrs. Miller's former names were Servos (birth name) and Brahm (her married name and my mother's maiden name). My mother's biological mother is unknown to me; from what my mother told me, she was the product of her father's relationship with a mistress.

I am hoping that there might be more documentation about Mrs. Miller or any other information that Rabbi Epstein may have gathered at that time.

One of my goals is to try to discover who my mother's biological mother was. I'm being cautiously optimistic about finding this but am trying every possible path that might lead me to more information.

I would be very grateful for any guidance you can provide or if there are archives from Rabbi Epstein's rabbinical offices that can be accessed at this time.

My thanks to you in advance for reading my story. My research journey has been fascinating, but provokes intense sadness about my family and the path they must have felt compelled to take to protect themselves from the unspeakable horrors of life in Europe at that time.

Best Regards,
Orlene

Tuesday, February 17, 2015
Dear Orlene Weyland,

I sincerely appreciate your communication. Alas, there is no way that I can be of assistance. Rabbi Epstein died in Jerusalem where he lived for the last thirty years of his life about nine years ago and I am not aware of his leaving any papers that might concern the matters that you raise. The Rabbi Jacob Joseph School certainly does not possess any such papers. In all candor, I am greatly surprised that he would have presided over a marriage ceremony.

With kindest wishes,
Marvin Schick

◊

Tuesday, February 17, 2015:
Thank you so much for your quick response. It is possible I am mistaken about Rabbi Epstein, but as the former address of the school and the address on my parent's marriage certificate were the same, it made me wonder. I am curious as to your thoughts about Rabbi Epstein in terms of his presiding over a marriage ceremony. Your observation intrigued me and any insight you can share would be greatly appreciated.

Thank you again for your consideration.
Orlene

◊

Wednesday, February 18, 2015:

Rabbi Epstein was not a rabbi of a congregation and I am not aware of him ever having performed a marriage ceremony.

This revelation came as a bit of a surprise. I will never know how this ceremony came about. I imagined the possibility that Rabbi Epstein was known, in some way, to my parents or to Irma Servos and her husband George Miller. It was time to move on in the research; sometimes you get to a place where the road has come to an end. In this case, I was not going to be able to discover anything more about the marriage ceremony or what Rabbi Epstein may have known about my parents.

Rabbi Schick's responsiveness is a valuable research lesson. Even when you are relentless in your search, you might not find what you are looking for. And as I discovered later on, being persistent often helps you find information that you wouldn't find otherwise.

Dad's Death and Mom's Descent Into Alzheimer's

MY RECOLLECTION is that when Dad passed away in July 1989, my sister and I were looking through some old papers in their safe (we may have been looking for a birth certificate or other document). I came across his medical school records and military documents and discovered that his religion was listed as Jewish. I also found the documentation of his name change in 1944; it was changed from Ladislav Adler to Larry (Leslie) Allen when he was in the British Army.

The author's father, Baltimore, Maryland Easter 1968

The records begged our questions of *why?*

Why had they not shared any of their experiences in Europe?

*Why did they avoid the questions we asked
about our family history?
Why did they embrace the concept of Jesus as
a teacher and prophet?
Why eschew the notion of him being the Son of God?
Why send us to Sunday school and raise us as Christians?
Why did they both wear crosses to display their
religious preference?
Why baptize Susie and me?*

The questions about our name were revealed in these documents, buried in a safe, never seen for so many years.

No other questions could be answered with these revelations and these were not discussions we could raise with Mom at this time.

◇

The period after Dad's death and Mom's rapid decline was a painful time for me and my sister and it was years before we opened up this discussion again.

◇

Prior to his death, Mom had bouts with what we would now characterize as depression and anxiety, some of which left her hospitalized. She was open to seeing a specialist but my father was not a believer in the benefits of mental health treatment (this was in the 1980s). So, he gave her small doses of valium to help with the anxiety and, from my perspective, completely denied the possibility of either mental illness or early dementia.

My mother developed serious food phobias prior to his death. She would only eat "white" foods, e.g., chicken, white bread, potatoes, rice, or ice cream (if my father made it). She stated that she was allergic to spices and that she would have vascular reactions if she ate, smelled, or kissed someone (my father) who had eaten almost any kind of seasoned food you could name. Her behavior became more peculiar; she carried her food supply in a cooler when they traveled to my sister's house. There she insisted on eating in the guestroom, because she couldn't tolerate the smell of any seasoned food that was being prepared in the kitchen. This led to serious gastrointestinal problems as well, which also left her hospitalized at least once. There was no hard medical evidence to support that anything was wrong with her gastrointestinal system, but the symptoms were described by her as "spasms" that were excruciatingly painful. She became a slave to the food phobias, which worsened after Dad died.

Following Dad's death, our involvement in Mom's life, health, and well-being became center stage. Discussion about our discovery was short-lived. Even after Mom's death in 1994, it took some time for my sister and me to even discuss the notion that Mom and Dad were Jewish. I shared what I knew with my daughter, even with the limited information I had. I didn't want this secret to pass through generations.

I can't recall if I asked my mother about this in the months following Dad's death. It is vague. The period after this loss was

---

ACTIVE TRANSLATION BUREAU
"ALL LANGUAGES, ALL SUBJECTS"
1472 BROADWAY
NEW YORK 18, N. Y.
(Page 2

TRANSLATION FROM SLOVAK:

Obligatory Subjects:

Religion (Jewish)	Very Good
Czechoslovak Language	Satisfactory
Latin Language	Satisfactory (on the bas of the oral examinatic
French Language	Satisfactory (on the bas of the oral examinatic
General History	Good
General Geography	Good
Civics	Good (on the basis of the oral examination)
Mathematics	Satisfactory
Zoology and Botany	Good (on the basis of the oral examination)
Chemistry and Mineralogy	Satisfactory
Geology	Very Good
Physics	Good
Descriptive Geometry	Satisfactory
Philosophical Propedeutics	Good
Gymnastics	Very Good

Non-Obligatory Subjects:

Laboratory of Experimental Physics	Very Good

Document discovered in father's safe: translation of secondary school completion in Bratislava. The document attests to his Jewish religion.

clouded with her profound grief, having lost her best friend, companion, lover, and provider. That's how she described him.

About a year after that (1990) my sister and I became increasingly concerned about her mental and physical health. Mom was also having psychotic breaks. A close friend living in her neighborhood was a mental health professional, and relayed her concerns to me. Mom was living in Peter Cooper Village in Manhattan, I was in Connecticut, and my sister lived in Maryland.

Mom would call me, sobbing and crying and saying she wanted to die. She was seeing a psychiatrist and told me she was having fantasies about him. She thought this meant she was getting better. I placed a call to him only to share my observations, not to ask for private information; no return call after multiple tries. Understanding the confidentiality issue, I felt completely frustrated with the lack of response from this physician, but had no option but to move on.

In 1991, we moved Mom to a lovely two-bedroom condominium in Maryland, not far from my sister's house. This arrangement didn't even last a year. She really couldn't live alone. She stayed with my sister on a periodic basis and the bouts of depression became worse, to the point where she was banging on walls screaming, "I want to die." Within a year she was hospitalized and we sadly agreed that the safest place for her was a nursing home. She lingered for two years, diagnosed with Alzheimer's.

The pain that Mom suffered and her description of her childhood and teen years, created a wish for me that she not die alone. Her stories of childhood abuse haunted me. I couldn't bear the thought that my wonderful, beautiful mother could be treated that way. Her fear of being abandoned became my fear for her. I couldn't bear the thought that she would die feeling alone and unloved. I would have felt that I had betrayed her.

To be with her when she was dying became an obsession and since I lived in Connecticut and she in Maryland at that time, it wasn't likely that I would be with her when it was time. The pain and anguish of watching her slip away from this dreadful, ugly disease was tearing me apart. I used to have nightmares of her dying alone and crying out for someone to love her and be with her. Sometimes the nightmares were present even during the day. So, as the universe plans for us, I got my wish.

With the help of an understanding and compassionate physician, my sister and I were able to grant him the task of letting her go in peace and with dignity. After two years in a nursing home, she died of early onset Alzheimer's at age 65.

Although Susie and I had very different relationships with Mom, we were in complete harmony that we wanted to be with her at the end. We knew that she wouldn't let go until her "girls" were together with her. We brought our parents' wedding rings for her to touch. We stayed with her, coached her, talked to her, and asked her to let go and be with Dad.

It was one of the most wrenching and moving experiences I have ever had. The feeling of closing Mom's eyes for the last time was an act of peaceful intimacy. We witnessed, heard, and felt the rhythm of death as it approached. And rhythmic it was; like sensing a deep but gentle wave that you know is going to dissipate when it reaches the sand.

The pain of losing my mom was devastating but I think she descended into profound grief when my dad died, complicated by the pace at which the Alzheimer's progressed. I believe that her early experiences with trauma, loss, and abuse were the contributors to her later depression, anxiety, and eating disorder. I wonder if these increased the rapid progression of Alzheimer's disease.

Twenty-six years after her death I have a different perspective on losing her. I miss her the most on my birthday. I have come to understand that while my time with her was shortened, I was lucky to have her for as long as I did. Not everyone gets that gift.

It's also joyful to me that she is with Dad in another place. Susie and I had what some would call visions, maybe some would call them delusions, when Mom was dying. At the last moment of life, both of us saw Dad with open welcoming arms and that smile; the one we used to see when he came home to greet Mom. He was motioning for her to come to him. We assured her we would be okay and that he needed her more than we did. And she slipped away to his open arms.

We talked about it later and were in disbelief that we had

both seen the same image. If I never believed in something in the afterlife, I do now. The vision was no delusion; it gave me the picture of joy that I associate with my mom and dad.

It also helped to dissipate some of the terrible images I had of my mom when she was so sick. Even though her brain and physical body were ravaged from the devastation of Alzheimer's, her deepest fears and expressions of being abandoned and abused still seemed to haunt her and, as such, they haunted me. It took some therapy and exposure to EMDR (Eye Movement Desensitization and Reprocessing) to help make those images less stark. I am still grateful to Alice Schumacher, M.S.W. in Middletown, Connecticut for helping me with that.

EMDR is a therapeutic treatment used to alleviate the distress associated with traumatic memories. I don't completely understand the neuroscience around how this works. With Alice's skillful guidance, the memory of Mom's face, so close up and distorted from the illness and weight loss - without a trace of who she was or what she ever looked like - exploded into millions of pieces, replaced with bright glowing lights. It's not that I don't remember how Mom's illness looked, but the constant close-up was gone. Over the years, this nightmarish picture has been replaced with the more beautiful memories of my mom.

Every time I look down at my left hand, I see the gold wedding ring that Mom held on to just before she died.

◊

When I remarried in 2011, I decided that mom's ring was good karma for my new marriage and it's also a wonderful daily reminder of her and my dad in their union.

◊

So, I got my wish, Mom didn't die alone. I am ever grateful for that.

Mom's Parents
Who Were They?

OSKAR ABRAHAM-BRAHM
JANUARY 12, 1892-1943

◇

IRMA SERVOS
JULY 17, 1899 - SEPTEMBER 2000

IN EARLY 2015, I clicked on to *ancestry.com,* not knowing that this would be the beginning of a complicated research process that became a significant focus of my day-to-day life. From the first finding, I felt compelled to keep going. Each new piece of information led to a labyrinth of questions, inquiries, and new findings.

What if I found nothing? What if I found the answers to my questions? What would I do with the information?

What started with a few strokes on a keyboard, led to a complicated research process. I had more questions, more speculation, more thinking in terms of possibilities, and more digging. It turned into hours, days, months, and now years, of searches, phone calls, letters, e-mails, and travel to places I never thought possible.

My first "hit" on *ancestry.com* was when I entered my mom's name, Eleonore Brahm. The first thing I saw was the record of her coming to the United States in 1948 on the S.S. America from Cherbourg, France. I thought my heart would jump out of my chest when I saw her name on the manifest.

But something wasn't right. She was listed as Eleonore Abraham-Brahm. Her maiden name was Brahm as far as I knew. The hyphenated name Abraham-Brahm made no sense to me. But I knew it was her. There was also a very small handwritten note next to her name that looked like it said, "D of line 30." Having

Passenger list indentifying the author's mother and her stepmother
(ancestry.com)

no idea what this meant, I made a random call to a representative at *Ancestry*. She was really helpful and suggested this might mean that Eleonore was the daughter (hence the D) of the individual named on line #30 of the document, Irma Millerova.

My heart began to pound; this was Irma Servos, her stepmother who had remarried (George Miller) and was now Irma Millerova. Parts of the puzzle were starting to come together with confirmation from the original marriage certificate that listed Irma Servos as her mother.

Having this information, my thoughts were to find out more about her father, Oskar Brahm. I searched through *ancestry. com* to no avail. It didn't make sense that I could find no record of him anywhere until I went to the United States Holocaust

Memorial Museum website. Still, I could find nothing through their search engine. I started to fill out one of their online research request forms and was having trouble filling it out so I called the museum.

As fate and good fortune would have it, I was connected to one of their researchers. In the fifteen or so minutes I talked to him, he had gone into their database and found my grandfather. The researcher spent a lot of time talking to me as he described the circumstance around Oskar Brahm's (known as Oskar Abraham-Brahm) death. He was murdered by the Nazis in 1943 after being deported from France.

This news, some fifty years later, instantly hit me with disbelief, grief, and anger all. I hung up the phone and went outside to get some fresh air, not knowing how to absorb this information. Overwhelming was just the beginning. I called my husband and sobbed this discovery to him. I called my sister; her initial response was what I would describe as a moment of silence, followed by, "I sort of figured that that's what happened." I don't know if it ever occurred to me that my grandfather had

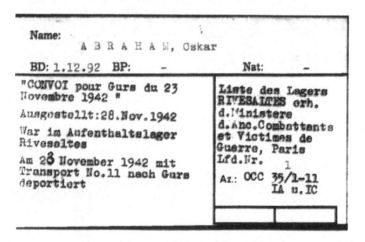

Oskar Abraham's deportation card,
courtesy of the U.S. Holocaust Memorial Museum

been exterminated by the Nazis. But my sister knew, even if she didn't have the facts.

The United States Holocaust Museum sent me a deportation

document that includes my grandfather and others who were deported from France to Majdanek in Southeast Poland in a portion of the country that was annexed by Germany at the beginning of World War II.

Oskar Abraham was murdered by the Nazis. As part of the news surrounding my grandfather's death, it still felt as though it had just happened and was yet another confirmation of his fate.

Upon further research, I was able to confirm that Oskar and Irma, along with my mom, were deported from Luxembourg

From the Mémorial de la Shoah, obtained by the author in 2019 during a visit to Paris. List of Holocaust victims displayed on the wall of the museum.
(Currently under renovation)

The deportation list containing Oskar Abraham-Brahm's name.
(Author's paternal grandfather)
Courtesy of the US Holocaust Memorial Museum, Washington, D.C.

to France on July 11, 1940. I have no additional information as to where Irma Brahm took my mom or how they were spared transport to one of the camps. Although this new documentation helped to uncover parts of the story, I experienced a sense of unreality about these discoveries. It takes time to digest the news even when the facts are in front of you.

I still had (and have to this day), questions about Oskar Abraham-Brahm that may never be answered. Based on what my mom told me, how could he have allowed his wife Irma to be so abusive to my mother? If my mother, as she described it,

The Central Database of Shoah Victims' Names

The Database includes data regarding Jews who were victims of persecution during the Holocaust period: those who were murdered as well as many others

Oscar Abraham

List from Yad Vashem Archives Scanned copy will be available shortly	Oscar Abraham was born in Trier, Germany in 1892. He was married Irma nee Servos. Prior to WWII he lived in Luxemburg, Luxembourg. During the war he was deported with Transport from Drancy,Camp,France to Majdanek,Camp,Poland on 04/03/1943. Oscar was murdered in the Shoah. This information is based on a Deportation list found in Lists of Jews from Luxemburg, 1940-1945.
Attach Image or Documentation	During the Shoah, Jews were murdered in a variety of ways, among them gassing, shooting, burning, drowning or burial alive, exhaustion through forced labor, starvation, epidemic diseases, deprivation of medical care and minimal hygienic conditions, and more.

Last Name:	Abraham
First Name:	Oscar
First Name:	Oskar
Gender:	Male
Date of Birth:	01/12/1892
Place of Birth:	Trier,Trier,Rhine Province,Germany
Marital Status:	MARRIED
Spouse's First Name:	Irma

tchfb.yadvashem.org/nam/es/namedDetails.html?itemId=7696195&lang.uage=en

Spouse's Maiden Name:	Servos
Permanent Place of Residence:	Luxembourg,Luxembourg
Deportation:	ל ורי ,France 07/11/1940 ב
Destination of Deportation:	France
Date of deportation:	07/11/1940
Details of transport:	Transport from ,Luxembourg to Vichy,Allier,France on 07/11/1940
Deportation:	n ורי Drancy,Camp,France ל Majdanek,Camp,Poland 04/03/1943 ב
Origin of Deportation:	Drancy,Camp,France
Destination of Deportation:	Majdanek,Camp,Poland
Date of deportation:	04/03/1943
Details of transport:	Transport from Drancy,Camp,France to Majdanek,Camp,Poland on 04/03/1943
Place of Death:	Majdanek,Camp,Poland
Date of Death:	06/03/1943
Cause of Death:	GAS CHAMBERS
Status in the source:	murdered
Related item:	Lists of Jews from Luxembourg, 1940-1945
Source:	Lists of Jews from Luxembourg, 1940-1945
Type of material:	Deportation list
Item ID:	7696195

* Indicates an automatic translation from Hebrew

The Names Database is a work in progress and may contain errors that will be corrected in the future.

From the Central Data Base of Shoah Victim's Names, Yad Vashem
(courtesy of the U.S. Holocaust Memorial Museum)

was the product of Oskar's relationship with a mistress, what, if anything, did Irma know about the other woman? Under what circumstance would she have agreed to take this child into her home? If Irma was involved in keeping my mother safe during the war, what means did she have to do this?

What if my mom's version of this story wasn't true? Having learned about my parents' Jewish history through their marriage certificate, how do I know that anything else I thought I knew about them is the true story?

MOM'S STEPMOTHER AND GEORGE MILLER

IRMA SERVOS
JULY 17, 1899–SEPTEMBER 2000

◇

GEORGE MILLER
APRIL 27, 1899–JANUARY 16, 1979

Irma Servos was Mom's stepmother. Married to Oskar Brahm, she raised my mom until he was deported in 1943. Mom was thirteen years old at the time and never saw him again. That was what she told me and my sister. She once said that he was in the French underground, but never elaborated on what that meant. Another time, she mentioned that he was a very successful businessman and hinted that he was wealthy. The glimpses and glimmers didn't add up to the full story of his fate. In retrospect, my sister had figured it out, but the topic was not open for questions or discussion with Mom or Dad, and Susie and I really didn't discuss it in our earlier years.

Mom described Irma as abusive and cruel. When Susie was born, Mom found out that Irma was not her biological mother and to add to the shock, she was told that she was the product of her father's relationship with his mistress. This is where Mom's description of Susie as the "blessing in disguise" fits in. We learned later on that Mom suffered a "breakdown" at that time and that Susie's birth was a gift, a lifeline, and gave her purpose.

Irma and my mother emigrated to the United States on April 8, 1948 on the "America" from the port of Cherbourg, France.

I don't know how they were able to leave Europe. They lived in Forest Hills, Queens, New York, along with Irma's second husband George Miller. I don't know how Irma and George met or where they were married. George Miller was born in Czechoslovakia and later emigrated to the United States. I wanted to know more about Irma, but the information was limited. I started with an internet search for naturalization records and came across the name Irma George Miller. Although the name didn't make sense, the combination of "Irma," "George," and "Miller" was worth pursuing.

That led me to the Find A Grave index where I discovered that Irma Miller was buried in the Mount Hebron Cemetery. On a wild hope, I called the cemetery to see if there might be more information about Irma, either on her headstone or in their records. They couldn't help me but referred me to the funeral home that handled her burial. I spoke to a woman who listened to my story and was more than willing to help me.

I was looking to confirm that this burial site was, in fact, Irma's, so I told her a little about the history and why I was looking for this information. I didn't think there was much to be found about Irma; I just wanted something concrete and real. I think I was still in a state of disbelief about everything I had discovered so far. It becomes surreal when you are surrounded by layers of what you know is the truth. Yet you keep looking for more truth and confirmation.

The woman from the funeral home said she would have to search the archives but would get back to me in a few days. What I didn't expect was a call just several hours later; this was the Irma Miller I was looking for. Her maiden name, Servos, was also contained in their records. She was buried next to her husband, George.

◊

At this writing, I have little interest in seeing Irma's grave, although I live only a few hours from Queens. I can't get past what my mom told me about this woman; why would I want to visit the grave of someone who was cruel and abusive? I want to understand Irma and forgive her, but I haven't discovered the path.

◊

I also wish I knew how Irma kept my mother (and herself) from being transported to a death camp. It is unlikely that I will find this information. I did more research on Irma and discovered that her parents, Albert and Laura Servos were both deported from Luxembourg in 1942 and murdered in Theresienstadt. (Source: YadVashem)

I also wondered about Irma's second husband, George Miller. I don't know where or under what circumstances she met him, but I wanted to find out more, in case there were children or other relatives who might have known Irma or anything else about her. Maybe these relatives even knew my mother! Although George and Irma were buried in Queens, they had lived in West Palm Beach, Florida where George died in 1979.

I wrote to the State of Florida for George's death certificate. I also found his obituary online, and Irma was listed as his sole survivor, so the chances of finding other relatives were slim.

I called the funeral home in Queens again and learned that there were no family members to be contacted about George or Irma, only an executor of their estate. Because of confidentiality laws, they were not able to give me the name of the executor. The same woman I was working with suggested that I write a letter to the executor; she would forward the letter on my behalf. I wrote the letter in November of 2015.

```
TO WHOM IT MAY CONCERN:
November 16, 2015

I am writing in the hopes that you or a repre-
sentative of the Miller family are open to talking
with me about my family history as it relates to
Mrs. Irma Miller (nee Servos).

I have been researching my family history
through a variety of sources since early this
year. I have been aware for quite some time that
Mrs. Miller raised my mother when she was mar-
ried to Oskar Abraham. (my maternal grandfather).
Through my research, I discovered that he was mur-
dered in Auschwitz in 1943.

Other information I have (verbal account) sug-
gests that Mrs. Miller was not my mother's biolog-
```

ical parent. Both my mother and Mrs. Miller survived the Holocaust. They were deported to France
from Luxembourg in 1940. My mother (Eleonore Allen
nee Abraham-Brahm) came to the United States in
1948 with Mrs. Miller and lived with her and Mr.
Miller (George) until 1949, when she married my
father. I never met Mrs. Miller, although I now
understand through my research that she resided in
Forest Hills, NY as well as West Palm Beach, FL. I
am not familiar with the circumstances under which
my mother and Mrs. Miller lost contact and to my
knowledge, they did not maintain a relationship.

I am hoping to learn more about Mrs. Miller, her
family and her life in Europe as well as here in
the United States. I am also hoping to gain information that might lead me to information about
my mother's birth mother if Mrs. Miller was not
her biological parent. If there are relatives or
others in Mrs. Miller's life who are willing to
talk with me, I would be most grateful.

I never got a response, but it was worth the calls and letters. You chase information until you know that you need to let it go. But it's always worth the chance; you never know what you might find or be led to. And maybe someday I will visit Irma's grave.

Ellen Schwarz

◇ TRUTH WITH UNEXPECTED DISCOVERIES ◇
◇ MOM'S BIRTH MOTHER ◇

ELLEN SCHWARZ may forever remain a mystery in this complicated puzzle. All I know is that my mom told me she was the product of a relationship between her father and his mistress. I don't know who told her this and the only guess I have would be Irma or possibly Blanche, although I have no reason to think that Blanche knew this.

Having discovered that Mom was born in Cologne, Germany (not France as she had told us), I learned that birth records in Germany are held by the city in which the birth occurred. My goal was to identify Mom's biological mother and see if I could uncover any more information as to this woman's possible relationship with my grandfather.

By now, having had some exposure to the process of obtaining birth records, as I had with my dad's birth records from Slovakia, I sent an e-mail inquiry to the City of Cologne. I started this process in January 2016 and through a series of e-mails, all of which were in German (thank goodness for Google translations), I discovered I would need to wire money to the City of Cologne for the request to be investigated. Through a long process and a series of mishaps (wiring money to Germany takes a lot of time, and it was difficult to find a bank that could do this), I finally received the document, after the first one got lost in the mail.

Of course, it was written in German, and thanks to a dear friend of my sister's and a later translation from a Connecticut company, I was able to make some sense of the hand-written notes on the document.

Prior to receiving the official document, the representative from Cologne shared the following (translated using Google):

- Eleonore Abraham was illegitimately born as Eleonore Schwarz.

- After adoption they received the name Brahm and later, by constitutional amendment the name Abraham. *

This was the affirmation I was seeking to confirm what my mom shared with me so many years ago. I thought this piece of the puzzle was solved; that I had found mom's birth mother and could put this to rest. I was not able to find any further information as to where Ellen Schwarz may have lived or under what circumstances she died. I decided that this was probably the end of this road.

Until I saw the literal translation of the document:

> The authorized officer of the Municipal Women's Hospital in Cologne-Lindenthal has reported that the unmarried Ellen Schwarz, no profession, residing in Cologne, has born a girl in Cologne-Lindenthat, in the aforementioned hospital on April fifteenth of the year one thousand nine hundred and twenty-nine, in the afternoon at a quarter past five, and that the child has been given the name Eleonore.

> By notarial contract of July 12, 1932, confirmed by the court on January 3, 1933, the spouses, merchant Oskar Braham and Irma nee Servos, both residing in Cologne, have adopted the child Eleonore Schwarz, as their own child. The child must bear the surname Brahm. She may not add this name to her previous name.

> And on March 27, 1940, in accordance with the Reich Minister of the Interior of October 7, 1939, the adoptive and parents and the child will bear the surname "Abraham" in place of the previous surname "Brahm" for reasons of sec. 7 of the Law on the Change of Surnames and First Names of January 5, 1938.

* Nazi Germany passed a law regulating approved names on January 5, 1938, "Second Regulation under the law re The changing of Family and Given names." The law provided for one list of names for ethnic Germans and another for Jews. See lbi.org/1938 projekt/on-this-day/; January 5.

I saw the word "adoption" and felt my heart pounding. I had never considered the possibility that mom could have been adopted. While her understanding of her birth circumstance was completely accurate, never did I hear that Oskar might not be her biological father. The birth record provided no clarity on this question. I was stunned. More questions without answers.

Adoption couldn't answer the question of Irma's cruel and abusive treatment of my mom. It doesn't explain why her father would have allowed this if he knew about it. It doesn't explain why a couple would choose to adopt a child and then have the child be abused. I'm not naïve enough to think this never happens; every day we hear about children who are in foster care, or are adopted, who are treated with neglect and cruelty. And if this were true, why would Irma (or someone else) have told my mother that she was the product of her father's relationship with his mistress? Was this also a lie? It would almost make sense if I imagined that Irma had agreed to take my mother as a baby, knowing that her husband created this child with his mistress. I can intellectually understand the resentment and anger that she may have felt about my mother, but can't process it emotionally. Did Irma lie about this? If she was capable of treating my mom with contempt and physical cruelty, no doubt she would have been capable of telling my mom this twisted misrepresentation of her birth.

Another question related to the information in this document is that of the time span between my mother's birth in 1929 and the actual adoption in 1932. There is no additional information on the birth document that would fill in this time gap.

◇ MORE DEAD ENDS ◇

I still wanted to know if Oskar Brahm was mom's biological father. Knowing that I was unlikely to find more information, I did some research with the hope of finding the hospital of her birth and found the University Hospital in Cologne. I am not sure it is the same institution today.

In May 2018, I sent an e-mail to the Municipal Women's Hospital in Cologne-Lindenthal to inquire of the possibility of locating archives and documents that might provide additional information about my mother's birth mother, clues to her biological father and the adoption. I was also hoping to find out where (and with whom) she lived from her birth in 1929 until 1932 when the adoption took place. To date I have not had a response.

Reaching another dead end was an agony. I won't give up, but I may have to move on. I still wonder where my mom spent the first few years of her life before she was adopted. I wonder if Oskar Brahm was Ellen Schwarz's lover and how she felt, giving birth to this beautiful baby and never having the privilege of loving and raising her.

I wonder if Oskar knew about the abuse and why he would allow his wife to treat a child with such cruelty and contempt. There is also wonder in my mom's innate ability to become a loving and nurturing mother to me and my sister. What is it that stops the cycle of abuse for some people and not others?

Today we might call this resilience. Knowing all that I know, resilience is a tame description for someone like my mom, who experienced catastrophic losses, abuse, abandonment, and loss of identity. How she was able to love, nurture and, through her mothering, teach me how to be a mother as well. This was a gift that came in a most complicated and secret package.

Copy of Eleonore Brahm's (author's mother) birth record.

Courtesy of the City of Cologne, Germany

Blanche Donath
Her Fate and Her Life

BLANCHE DONATH
FEBRUARY 21, 1906–JULY 29, 2005

◇

ZOLTAN DONATH
MAY 10, 1914–JULY 9, 1942

BLANCHE WAS still a mystery in terms of what had happened in her relationship with Mom and Dad. Sometime during the 1960s we no longer had contact with her. My recollection was that Blanche was actively involved in our lives, even when we lived in different parts of the country. I recall her visits to wherever we lived and we also visited her in the Bronx.

Blanche's first husband and her life in Europe were completely unknown to us. All we knew is that she was a widow and did not have children. She used to talk about a man named Tony, who was her boyfriend, but my sister and I never met him. She was a seamstress and traveled to the garment district on the subway from the Bronx every day.

What a stark difference from the way our family lived. Dad was a successful physician and we lacked nothing. We lived in beautiful houses or apartments, went on many vacations and got to see the United States from one side of the country to the other. We were loved and cared for. Mom, Susie, and I were the center of Dad's world. What a contrast to what may have been a lonely existence for Blanche and the hard work she did in the garment district.

Somewhere around the mid-1960s, we heard nothing else about Blanche from Mom and Dad. There was no contact that I recall, and any mention of her to Mom and Dad was not positively received. The little bit of discussion I heard some years later was that she had reported, or had threatened to report,

Blanche in later years (dates unknown)
discovered in Blanche's apartment after her death.

Dad to the U.S. Government as being connected to the Communist Party during the McCarthy era. If that were true, this was not something to be ignored during that time in history. It would be understandable that she and my father would not be on speaking terms.

I really don't know if this happened and I have not been able to identify a research path that might lead me to this information. I include it as part of my story as a possible explanation for their severed relationship. The message at home was that she was not to be mentioned.

◊

Information discovered later on in the research suggests a different possibility in terms of why their relationship may have been terminated. This later discovery also documents that Blanche spoke of not having family here in the United States.

◊

I went back to *ancestry.com* and found Blanche's application for naturalization in the United States, as well as the date and place of her death in 2005 at the age of 99. I was surprised to see that she had lived such a long life and that she had moved to Sunny Isles, Florida. Even with this little bit of information, I felt deep regret that it was only now that I had learned of this. It felt like a lost opportunity to learn the answers to so many questions I had about her, my father, and the rest of my family.

At that time, I was using the U.S. Holocaust Memorial Museum website search function. In a search request to discover more about my paternal grandparents (Jakub and Julia Adler), I made a connection with another one of their researchers. While they were not able to find documentation about my grandparents, they were able to find archived documents about Blanche and her first husband Zoltan. This was the first time I knew his name.

The research staff at the U.S. Holocaust Memorial Museum

Zoltan (left); Blanche and Zoltan Donath (right) date unknown, discovered in Blanche's apartment after her death.

in Washington, D.C. has been a treasure in terms of their tireless efforts to research my family and provide answers to so many questions. They have supported me both at the informational level and emotionally beyond my wildest expectations.

In October 2015, my husband and I drove to Washington D.C. to review their findings.

The discovery was gut wrenching. Blanche survived four

Copy of Blanche's time in concentration camps
(courtesy of the U.S. Holocaust Memorial Museum)

concentration camps, Auschwitz, Kurzbach, Gross-Rosen, and Bergen-Belsen, beginning in 1944. She was liberated in April of 1945. Her husband, Zoltan, was murdered during a transport to Auschwitz in 1942.

Although my aunt never spoke about him, I still can't imagine what this experience did to her. I later obtained documents (2016) in the form of an assessment performed by a physician in New York City. Blanche was applying for restitution from

Copy of Blanche's alien registration card (ancestry.com)

the German government as a Holocaust survivor. At the time of the evaluation, she was 59 years old.

Below is the translated evaluation performed on February 12, 1965 by John Taterka, M.D.:

> Mrs. D. was married on April 29, 1940. Her husband, parents, and two siblings* perished during the persecution.
>
> During Spring of 1939 Mrs. D. was in a Ghetto and then was sent to several concentration camps. During her detainment, she was forced to do hard labor and was mistreated several times. Once she was hit with a whip on the right side of the head and face and since then she suffers pain in both head and face.
>
> While in Bergen-Belsen she contracted typhoid fever
>
> She attended school here, learned draping and was working in a clothing factory.
>
> Mrs. D. suffers from insomnia, depression, nightmares from the camp. She is easily irritated, has problems to control herself, fights with her employer and coworkers. Her current employers know her circumstances and make allowances.
>
> Furthermore, she suffers headaches, dizziness and neuralgia in the right side of the face. Mrs. D. does not have family here** and very few friends, she often feels lonely. She never attempted to get married again.

*My sister and I were led to believe that there was one sibling who perished during the persecution, perhaps the brother who "died in the war." We had no knowledge of another sibling.

**Blanche reported that she had no family here in the U.S. This statement was made around the same time that her relationship with our dad was severed.

◇

The feelings of grief and devastation were starting to feel familiar; it is difficult to describe the experience of discovering that so many in your family were tortured or murdered at the hands of the Nazis.

◇

Having this information about my aunt made it hard to escape the thoughts and images of her experience. It is unimaginable that millions of people suffered such heinous treatment, and yet it is the truth.

the mental health association
of Westchester County, Inc.
29 STERLING AVE., WHITE PLAINS, N. Y.

Bell Ringer Office
WH 6-0960

Dearest Blanche,
please forgive me for the
delay - I had a very crazy week - hope
all is well - thanks again for a lovely
afternoon - hope to see you (and Toni)
in our house real soon - please give
my regards to Toni (hope he doesn't mind
my calling him by his first name)

love to you

3/10/61

Letter to Blanche discovered after her death.
Believed to be written by the author's father.

Topoľčany, Slovakia:
Looking for Adler/Schlesinger Families

JAKOB ADLER
MARCH 5, 1863-UNKNOWN

◇

JULIA (SCHLESINGER) ADLER
NOVEMBER 13, 1873-UNKNOWN

PART OF my research involving the U.S. Holocaust Memorial Museum was to discover information about my paternal grandparents, Jakub and Julia (Schlesinger) Adler. The Museum's search function revealed no information; I tried other sources, e.g., JewishGen.org, Yad Vashem, but to no avail.

The author's paternal grandparents, Jakob Adler and Julia Schlesinger Adler
(dates unknown)

With the little information I had, I researched Yizkor books from Topoľčany, Czechoslovakia as well. Yizkor books are memorial books commemorating a Jewish community destroyed in the Holocaust. The books are published by former residents or societies as remembrances of homes, people, and ways of life lost during World War II. Yizkor books usually focus on a town, but may include sections on neighboring smaller communities. Most of these books are written in Yiddish or Hebrew; some provide parts in English or other languages, depending on where they were published. Since the 1990s, many of these books, or sections of them, have been translated into English.

I found their surnames in the Yizkor book from Topoľčany. I scanned the list of the Adler and Schlesinger names, but could not confirm their identities. One listing for a female with the name Adler did not provide a first name, but listed Jakub as the spouse. Jakub Adler was listed twice but no other information. If these were my grandparents, I would know they had been murdered in the Holocaust.

The Adler and Schlesinger names were common in Topoľčany but I had no information about their dates of birth, which would be needed to discover any additional information. What seemed like another dead end led to another possibility.

The museum suggested I contact the Slovak embassy to see if I could obtain Dad's birth certificate; surely it would have his parents' dates of birth. I placed a call to the New York Office and submitted my request to the Consulate General of the Slovak Republic. Within six weeks I had the document. It only listed their ages at the time Dad was born in 1914; no specific dates. I was disappointed, as I thought this was the path to the information I was seeking. Not a complete dead end but a place to start.

◇ SEEING DAD'S BIRTHPLACE ◇

John and I were planning a trip to Prague for the spring of 2016. In anticipation of this, I talked to another researcher at the U.S. Holocaust Memorial Museum. Even with my grandparents' approximate birth years, she wasn't able to find any documentation about them.

SLOVENSKÁ REPUBLIKA

RODNÝ LIST

Č.:

V knihe narodení matričného úradu		Bojná			
zväzok 3	ročník 1914	strana 206	por.č.	163	je zapísané

Deň, mesiac, rok narodenia a rodné číslo	3.12.1914 - tretí december jedentisíc deväťsto štrnásť		neuvedené
Miesto narodenia	Malé Dvorany		
Meno a priezvisko	**Ladislav Adler**		
Pohlavie	mužské		
Otec — Meno a priezvisko, rodné priezvisko, deň, mesiac, rok a miesto narodenia, štátne občianstvo, rodné číslo	Jakob Adler rod.Adler 51 Slovenskej republiky		neuvedené
Matka — Meno a priezvisko, rodné priezvisko, deň, mesiac, rok a miesto narodenia, štátne občianstvo, rodné číslo	Julia Adler rod.Schlesinger 42 Slovenskej republiky		neuvedené
Poznámky			

V Bojnej

dňa 23.novembra 2015

meno a priezvisko matrikára

podpis

T MV SR 27-004   I/2011   0618901

Birth Certificate of Ladislav Adler, the author's father, obtained by the author through the Slovak Embassy.

She connected me to a researcher at the University of Bratislava Holocaust Documentation Center. Dr. Jan Hlavinka, whom I communicated with for several months beginning in February 2016 through April 2016. Dr. Hlavinka was instrumental in finding the last known location for Jakub and Julia Adler and providing some possible scenarios as to their eventual fate.

He also named the last known location for them in the town

of Žilina, Slovakia (less than 100 miles from Topoľčany where the Adler family lived). I was getting closer to finding the truth, knowing the outcome would be grim. Once more, I needed something concrete, to link their names with what I knew was their likely fate.

◇

February 2016

Good afternoon Dr. Hlavinka, I am writing to you at the suggestion of Michlean Lowy Amir from the United States Holocaust Museum in Washington D. C.

She thought that you might be a very good resource to provide some guidance in terms of my family research pertaining to my father's side of my family.

The following provides some brief background and information I am seeking:

My father (Ladislav Adler) was born in Topoľčany, Slovakia on December 3, 1914. He was educated at the University Bratislava Medical School, graduating in 1939 and serving in the British Army until 1946. It is not clear to me as to how he left the country to go to England or the circumstances surrounding his departure. My father came to the United States after World War II and spent the rest of his life here, practicing medicine until he passed away in 1989.

The information I am seeking is related to his parents, Jakob Adler (born in 1863) and Julia Adler (born in 1872) nee Schlesinger. (This information is from my father's birth certificate, which I obtained through the Slovak Embassy). I have not been able to find any confirmed record of what happened to them or when they died. I have used ancestry.com, Jewishishgen.org, the United States Holocaust Museum databases, yadvashem.org, and familysearch.org. and have not found documentation that can verify what I am looking for.

The only information I have found is from the Yizkor book from Topoľčany, which lists two individuals named Jakub Adler. One listing for a female with the name Adler does not provide a first name, but states that the spouse's name was Jakub. Based on this information I am not able to verify if these are my grandparents. If it would be helpful to you, I can scan and send you this document.

Below is some information that I hope will be helpful:

My father, Ladislav Adler born in 1914 (youngest of the four children) Topoľčany. His siblings were:

Blanche (Blanka) Donath (nee Adler) born in 1906. Blanche was a survivor of the Bergen-Belsen concentration camp. She came to the U.S. after World War II. Her husband Zoltan (born in 1914 in Zelina) was shot in transport to Auschwitz in 1942 (this information came from the International Tracing Services file that Michlean was able to locate). I am not aware if she had any children.

Kamila Adler: Kamila was married but I do not have her married name and was told that she had a son named Peter who died at the age of 13. I am not able to verify this information about her son.

A brother whose name I do not know but was told he died in the war.

I have written to Professor Pavol Mestan at the Museum of Jewish Culture in Bratislava as well as the mayor of Topoľčany Mr. Peter Balaz. As of this writing, I have not received a response.

I apologize for the lengthy e-mail I am sending; I am hoping you can guide me as to where I might find additional records of Jakub and Julia Adler. If it would be helpful for us to talk by phone, please let me know what your availability might be. My experience has been that talking with research experts is invaluable in uncovering information.

I will be in Prague the week of April 18, 2016

and am hoping to go to Bratislava and Topoľčany while I am there. If meeting with you would provide some guidance, please let me know if you are available.

Many thanks in advance for your help.

◇

April 2016: Dr. Hlavinka's Response

I hereby send you the preliminary results of the research pertaining Jakub Adler and Julia Adler:

1. Jakub Adler, born on March 5, 1863 in "Bystrica n/T" (the exact name of the place is still unknown, the info was transcripted from the archival document) was recorded as the inhabitant of town of Zilina (Žilina), Slovakia in Spring 1944. He lived at the that time at Orolska 2 Street, occupation: pensioner (retired person). This means Jakub Adler was not deported from Slovakia during the deportations of Jews from Slovakia in 1942. We do not have any other records pertaining to Jakub Adler.

2. Julia Adler, nee Schlesinger was born on November 13, 1873 in Ludanice, she was recorded in 1942 as the inhabitant of Hlohovec, Slovakia and in Spring 1944 as the inhabitant of Zilina (also) at Orolska 2 Street.

This information comes from our database which is the result of the transcription of specific archival documents (Jewish Census 1942, Jewish Census 1944, Transport lists 1942 etc.) stored in Slovak National Archives. However, our center does not have the source documents for above-mentioned records available and can only obtain those in Slovak National Archives.

Based on this I would recommend to conduct further research and to focus it at:

1. The question whether both Jakub and Julia Adler were deported from Slovakia during period Fall 1944 - Spring 1945 (so called "second wave of deportations") and if so, where they were deported. Such research can be based on the records of the International Tracing Service (ITS), Bad Arolsen,

Germany, available also at the United States Holocaust Memorial Museum, Washington, D.C., USA.

2. The question whether both Jakub and Julia Adler could possibly become victims of a mass murder committed by the members of some Einsatzkommando and/or Hlinka Guard unit during the period Fall 1944 - Spring 1945 at the territory of Slovakia. However, in order to verify this possibility, the long-term research of various sources stored in various archives has to be conducted.

◇

I wrote an e-mail to the Mayor of Topoľčany, hoping he might have archival information about my grandparents or provide some guidance and direction. Unfortunately, I didn't hear back from him. I think the language barrier may have prevented him from answering my e-mail.

I wanted to go to Topoľčany and bear witness to the place that Dad came from. I wanted to find out about his parents and anyone else in the Adler/Schlesinger family who lived in the town. My contact at the U.S. Holocaust Memorial Museum connected me to the Magni Tour company in Prague, with whom John and I arranged for a two-day trip to Topoľčany as part of our stay.

What a treasure the Magni Tour company was!

I don't speak Czech and it would have been impossible to navigate the five-hour drive, as well as communicate with anyone we might meet. The owner of Magni Tours arranged to come to our rental apartment when we arrived in Prague with a proposed agenda, and also to talk with us about what we hoped to accomplish in this trip to Topoľčany. We arrived in Prague on Monday morning and went to our beautiful rental apartment on the quiet side of the Charles Bridge. What a view!

On Tuesday evening, Marek from Magni Tours arrived and walked us through the itinerary he had developed. The trip would take about five hours each way. We would also stop in Trebic for a walking tour to see the Jewish Quarter, the old Jewish cemetery and the Basilica of St. Procopius.

We left early Wednesday morning with the driver, George, and translator/guide Michaela. George was a large man with a gentle face who spoke minimal English. His demeanor was friendly and helpful and I knew we were in the right hands. Michaela was a small and tightly built woman whose presence was intense and purposeful. Here was a woman who could take charge of a situation and lead. Without George and Michaela, we could not have had such a meaningful journey to my dad's birthplace.

I was excited and anxious about the trip. I had such hope to find more information about the Adler and Schlesinger families. In particular, information about my grandparents, Julia and Jakob.

We stopped at Trebic, several hours outside of Prague. This city, its houses in the former ghetto, the Jewish Cemetery and Basilica of St. Procopius, have been included in the UNESCO World Natural Heritage Site list. It was the first independent Jewish monument to be honored that is outside of the state of Israel.

We stopped there for lunch and a quick tour. I don't remember very much about the tour; my focus was getting to Topoľčany and I was getting more and more anxious about what we might find.

As we approached Topoľčany, I saw miles and miles of rapeseed. Beautiful, yellow vegetation that contrasted with the bright blue sky. It looked like a picture from a tour book.

My imaginary and uneducated vision of Topoľčany as a beautiful rural hamlet quickly vanished when we arrived there. The streets were deserted. You could count the number of people with one hand. The buildings were old and dilapidated. I felt an eerie sense of a place that had been forgotten by time.

We went to the hotel that Marek had booked for us. He told us it was the best place in town. It was simple in its Ikea-like decor, but it was very clean and the staff were friendly in spite of the language barrier.

We entered the bar in the lobby of the hotel; John and I had a glass of wine while Michaela texted with her children. George sat with a coffee and a cigarette. We were all trying to get our bearings. I looked around the bar and noticed the big screen television. Nothing unusual, but we were seeing videos of Michael Jackson that were from the 1980s. Remember "Billie Jean"? Another eerie sense of a place that time had forgotten.

John and I took a walk later that afternoon into the town square. The absence of people was remarkable to me. What once may have been a bustling center of activity looked desolate. Later on, our guide found a restaurant for us not far from the hotel. John and I went there to celebrate his 69th birthday. The place was old, well maintained, and the food was delicious. For my culinary tastes, schnitzel and dumplings are one of the best attractions in Eastern Europe. I feel at home when I eat it or attempt to cook it.

When we left to return to our hotel, it was dark and once again, there was no one in view. I felt very nervous, not knowing our surroundings and having no ability to speak the language. My dear husband found our way back to the hotel and we fell into bed, exhausted. The next morning, we rose early and met George and Michaela.

We drove to the town center where the administrative offices were housed. Michaela spoke to a gentleman we met outside of the building who directed us to the administrative offices inside.

Topoľčany town hall, visited by the author in 2016
Photo by Dr. János Korom, on wikipedia.com

With no appointment, we had no idea if someone would see us or talk to us. Michaela strode in with confidence, purpose, and a level of chutzpah I had never witnessed. Several minutes later, two women from the back office ushered us in and stopped everything they were doing to help us. They went into the archives (which were housed in another part of the building) and

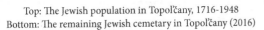

Počet židov v Topoľčanoch

Rok	Počet obyvateľov	Počet židov	%
1716	-	14 rodín	-
1744	-	1 rodina	-
1768	-	56	-
1787	1 926	120	6, 2
1828	2 475	561	22, 7
1842	3 113	680	21, 8
1880	3 689	1 120	30, 4
1900	4 944	1 676	33, 9
1919	7 023	1 954	27, 8
1921	7 238	1 974	27, 3
1930	8 731	2 192	25, 1
1940	10 242	2 459	24, 0
1948	8 857	344	3, 9

Top: The Jewish population in Topoľčany, 1716-1948
Bottom: The remaining Jewish cemetary in Topoľčany (2016)

Veľká synagóga v Topoľčanoch

Ruina topoľčianskej Veľkej synagógy
tesne po vojne

Pictures of pre and post-Nazi devasation to the synagogue in Topoľčany

brought back volumes of large, heavy record books containing documentation of land ownership. We pored over them but could not find land ownership records of Julia and Jakob.

I asked about the address I had for Julia and Jakob in Žilina, naively thinking they may have moved there after my dad left the country in 1939. As they spoke to Michaela in Slovak, their faces softened and they looked reluctant to speak. My heart was pounding as it was clear to me that they wanted to tell me something but it did not look like it was going to be good news. I was still clinging to the hope that my grandparents had died of natural causes. Instead, through Michaela, they told me that Žilina was a holding station for Jews to be transported to the camps. Once again, my family's truth was bared.

The starkness of this truth is completely devastating when you hear it aloud, in words, even if the words are in a foreign language.

Shared grief had no language barrier that day. These two women wept with me as I took the news in. As I returned to the car, my thoughts were spinning. I felt as sad as I did the day I found out that my maternal grandfather had been murdered by the Nazis.

Note: later research uncovered my grandparents names on a list of Holocaust victims from Žilina: Haim Gordon ,"The Rise and Decline of the Jewish Commuinity of Žilina," Printed in Jerusalem, 2003

Even with all I learned in Topoľčany and the scenarios presented by the University of Bratislava about my grandparents, there is still a level of disbelief when the fragments of your family secrets come to light.

With this devastating discovery swirling around me like a dark and ominous cloud, I began to feel something else. I was experiencing a profound sense of gratitude for the kindness and sensitivity bestowed upon me by these two women. I will never forget their kind faces and soft words of understanding.

We continued our trip through Topoľčany, stopping at the entrance to the only Jewish cemetery in the town. No one was there, but there was evidence of a caretaker whose name and number were posted on a sign on the gate.

Priezvisko	Meno	Dátum narodenia	Dátum a miesto transportu		Dátum a miesto úmrtia
Adler	Adolf	1912	31.03.1942	Majdanek	
Adler	Adolf	31.10.1936	03.07.1942	Auschwitz	
Adler	Akacz	31.03.1924	31.03.1942	Majdanek	
Adler	Akoš	21.03.1915			*02.02.1945 Buchenwald
Adler	Alfred	1925	31.03.1942	Majdanek	
Adler	Alojz	30.08.1896	03.07.1942	Auschwitz	*06.07.1942 Auschwitz
Adler	David	30.11.1927	03.07.1942	Auschwitz	
Adler	Emil	08.09.1935	03.07.1942	Auschwitz	
Adler	Ervin	25.05.1928	22.04.1942	Opole	
Adler	Eugen	1908			
Adler	Fridrich	1904	31.03.1942	Majdanek	
Adler	Gustáv	31.08.1931	03.07.1942	Auschwitz	
Adler	Heinrich	14.02.1894	03.07.1942	Auschwitz	
Adler	Hermann	26.09.1864	22.04.1942	Opole	
Adler	Ignác	01.04.1923	31.03.1942	Majdanek	
Adler	Jakub	07.01.1894	22.09.1942	Auschwitz	*05.01.1945 Auschwitz
Adler	Jakub	1916	1942		
Adler	Jozef	10.10.1899	22.04.1942	Opole	
Adler	Július	1922	31.03.1942	Majdanek	
Adler	Karol	11.10.1929	22.04.1942	Opole	
Adler	Leopold	24.05.1877	22.04.1942	Opole	
Adler	Maximilian	26.03.1927	22.04.1942	Opole	
Adler	Michal	11.12.1941	03.07.1942	Auschwitz	
Adler	Richard	01.06.1908	24.07.1942	Auschwitz	
Adler	Samuel	26.10.1914	19.04.1942	Auschwitz	*21.07.1942 Auschwitz
Adler	Samuel	1924	27.07.1942	Majdanek	
Adler	Edita	29.09.1935	03.07.1942	Auschwitz	
Adler	Ernst	1898	20.10.1942	Auschwitz	
Adler	Eva	28.08.1940	03.07.1942	Auschwitz	
Adler	Františka	10.11.1896	03.07.1942	Auschwitz	
Adler	Gizela	08.05.1906	22.04.1942	Opole	
Adler	Hedviga	03.07.1927	03.07.1942	Auschwitz	
Adler	Johana	14.03.1932	03.07.1942	Auschwitz	
Adler	Júlia	06.02.1888	22.04.1942	Opole	
Adler	Katarína	20.08.1881	22.04.1942	Opole	
Adler	Lea	08.07.1912	03.04.1942	

Priezvisko	Meno	Dátum narodenia	Dátum a miesto transportu		Dátum a miesto úmrtia
Schlesinger	Cecília	11.07.1897			*21.11.1944 Kremnička
Schlesinger	Edita	02.04.1918	19.04.1942	Auschwitz	*18.08.1942 Auschwitz
Schlesinger	Ela	1898	13.04.1942	Auschwitz	
Schlesinger	Fany	1868	18.09.1942	Auschwitz	
Schlesinger	Frederika	27.05.1903	30.09.1944	Auschwitz	
Schlesinger	Gertrúda				
Schlesinger	Gizela	11.10.1905	22.04.1942	Opole	
Schlesinger	Gizela	07.11.1908	30.09.1944	Auschwitz	
Schlesinger	Hedviga				
Schlesinger	Hermína	13.06.1901	19.06.1942	Auschwitz	*18.08.1942 Auschwitz
Schlesinger	Janetta	12.12.1887	22.04.1942	Opole	
Schlesinger	Leopoldína	02.01.1890	19.04.1942	Auschwitz	*29.09.1942 Auschwitz
Schlesinger	Lily	1939	19.09.1942	Auschwitz	
Schlesinger	Magda	17.03.1921	19.04.1942	Auschwitz	*15.08.1942 Auschwitz
Schlesinger	Malvína	10.10.1862	10.07.1942	Auschwitz	
Schlesinger	Marta	1907	17.07.1942	Auschwitz	
Schlesinger	Melánia				
Schlesinger	Mina	25.01.1870	11.06.1942	Sobibor	
Schlesinger	Regína	1904	19.04.1942	Auschwitz	
Schlesinger	Renata	20.03.1928	17.07.1942	Auschwitz	
Schlesinger	Renata	11.03.1941	31.07.1942	Auschwitz	
Schlesinger	Rozália	1899			*1944 Slovakia
Schlesinger	Šarlota	30.10.1899			*21.11.1944 Kremnička
Schlesinger	Stela	30.07.1927			*21.11.1944 Kremnička
Schlesinger	Valeria	31.01.1913			*21.11.1944 Kremnička
Schlesinger	Vilma	1902	31.07.1942	Auschwitz	
Schlössler	Richard	08.03.1905	19.04.1942	Auschwitz	*12.07.1942 Auschwitz
Schlössler	Rudolf				
Schlössler	Ester				
Schmid	Ferdinand	11.09.1930	17.07.1942	Auschwitz	
Schmid	Johana	29.08.1923	02.04.1942	Auschwitz	
Schmiedel	Ferdinand	11.11.1924	14.06.1942	Majdanek	
Schmiedel	Heinrich	18.08.1896	14.06.1942	Majdanek	
Schmiedel	Jozef	15.03.1856	14.06.1942	Sobibor	
Schmiedel	Ludovít	22.11.1920	31.03.1942	Majdanek	
Schmiedel	Janka	23.04.1894	14.06.1942	Sobibor	

Lists of the Adler and Schlesinger families
who perished in the Holocaust (Topoľčany) (visited by author in 2016)

Michaela insisted on calling him and within minutes, he appeared at the gate, ready to help. He showed us through the cemetery, explaining through Michaela that it was rarely used or visited anymore.

He took us to a small building that was now the home of an exhibit produced by the local high school. The old house is where he lived when he was growing up. As we looked at the exhibit, I was overcome by the pictures and documents displayed here. One of them was a document that described the percentage of Jewish townspeople before and after the Holocaust. The population decline of the Jewish community had plummeted from twenty four percent to under four percent during the catastrophic Nazi era.

There were pictures of Topoľčany before the Nazi regime, especially one of the synagogue, which, in its prime, was a beautiful house of worship. The post-Nazi pictures were only a glimpse of the destruction; the building was burned beyond recognition.

There were pictures of Topoľčany families, many who bore the same surnames as my grandparents. The caretaker told us that the Adler/Schlesinger names were very common in the town, so it is possible that I may be distantly related to some of them.

We looked at documents and lists of townspeople who were deported and transported to the camps. After searching through the Adler/Schlesinger names, I could not find any that bore the names of my grandparents. Knowing what I had found out at the town offices, I felt the same intense grief for this town and its people.

From there, we went to the town funeral home, hoping to find records of others in my family. In the same spirit as the town administrators and the cemetery caretaker, the funeral home director stopped what he was doing and went to his records. Nothing indicated that anyone in my family was buried in Topoľčany, just more depressing information and the physical evidence that few survived the Nazis.

Zoznam žilinských obetí holokaustu

Z Žilina Gallery Wiki

Obsah

Zoznam žilinských obetí holokaustu

רשימה שמית של קורבנות השואה מז'ילינה

The Holocaust victims of Žilina

Die Holocaust Opfer von Sillein

Ableser Samuel, Ableser Ružena, Ableser Bernát, Ableser Margita, Adler Alica, **Adler Jakob, Julia,** Adler Armin. Adler Edita, Adler Roland, **Adler Julia,** Adler Jozef, Adler Leo, Adler Eugen, Adler Hermina, Adler Eva, Alt Mariena, Alt František, Alt Viliam, Altmann Koloman, Altmann Cecilia, Altmann Robert, Altmann Blanka, Altmann Pavel, Altmann Ida, Altmann Samuel, Altmann Róza, Altmann Marcel Dr., Altmann Robert-Poldi, Apfelmann V

Richard, Auerbach Margita, Auerbach Evelina, Auerbach Edita, Auerbach Arnošt, Axelrad Klára,

Partial list of the Holocaust victims from Zilina (Jakub and Julia Adler)
http://Zilina-gallery.sk/wiki/Zoznam

◇ ELLA ADLER ◇

NOVEMBER 27, 1904 - JULY 30, 1940

We searched for possible records of Ella Adler. I had a picture of her grave that was discovered later in the research along with other pictures and documents related to our family.

Ella Adler was born in Topoľčany and it is possible that she was buried here. The funeral director told us that it was likely that her grave had been destroyed, or that other coffins were buried over it, a common practice at one time.

Ella Adler must be related to us in some way but we will probably never know. Could she have been the wife of Dad's

Ella Adler's grave (picture discovered in Blanche's apartment after her death)

brother (name unknown to us) who died in the war? Could she have been a sibling that he never spoke of? Could Dad have been married before he left Slovakia in 1939? I was back in the mode of endless possibilities, not wanting to give in to what could be a dead end. It is unlikely that we will find out how Ella Adler fit into our family. I hold that thought for future research.

We thanked the funeral director and went on our way. As we drove through the streets, we passed what looked like an old school building or apartments that looked like tenements. I saw children playing outside of the building but as I looked closer, I could see them playing in pools of filthy water and dressed in ragged clothes. They looked hungry and thin.

Michaela was horrified; she explained that Roma populations, sometimes referred to as "gypsies" still existed in Slovakia. I use the description "gypsies" while understanding that this is a negative and disparaging word that has been used by majority populations to describe the Roma people.

Early in this century, the Roma in Slovakia, as elsewhere in Europe, formed an ethnic community, living on the social periphery of the mainstream population. State policy nearly always focused on the Romany population not as a distinct ethnic minority, but rather perceived them as a particularly anti-social and criminal group. This attitude was reflected in a policy to obtain special police evidence in the form of fingerprint collections of members of Romany groups (1925), a law about wandering Roma (1927), and so on. During the Second World War, approximately six to seven thousand Roma from Bohemia and Moravia died in a special concentration camp at Auschwitz. The Slovak State also copied the racist legislation of the German Reich, establishing special labor camps for the Roma. They were also forbidden to travel with public transport, were allowed admission to towns and communities only on limited days and hours, had their settlement units separated from public roads, and so on. After the occupation of Slovakia by the German army, mass killings of Roma occurred in many places.

Source: Slovakia.Org, Roma in Slovakia, Klara Orgovanova

Michaela's reference to the Roma people as "gypsies" reminded me of a story my dad told me a long time ago.

His mother was frantic because she couldn't find him as he had wandered a little too far from their home. She thought he had been taken away by the gypsies. I don't know what that meant to him as a child; he told the story in a way that wouldn't have made the listener feel afraid. He didn't explain the Roma population to me or that they were considered criminal or dangerous. Surely he knew that as an adult. Maybe it was another way of hiding his story.

On our way out of Topoľčany, we drove through the section or hamlet, called Malé Dvorany, where my dad and his siblings were raised. There was little there: crumbling buildings, one that may have been a factory, but no signs of people or recovery from the destruction that occurred more than seventy years ago.

On our way back to Prague, I asked George if we could stop in Bratislava. I had the address where Aunt Kamila lived until her death in 1990 at 2 Budovatelska Street. We found the apartment building in a pretty, tree-lined neighborhood. The building was very tall and grey and looked as though its age had finally caught up with it. The neighborhood reminded me of Peter Cooper Village in Manhattan, where Mom and Dad used

2 Budovatelska Street, Bratislava, Slovakia (home of the author's Aunt Kamila)
visited by the author in 2016

to live. We got a quick look at the new "Old Town Bratislava" before we left, stopped for a coffee and some sweets, and then we were on our way back to Prague.

I still think about a question that Michaela posed to me on the drive back to Prague. She asked me what it meant to me to be a Jew. I didn't respond immediately, as I wasn't sure what she meant. Based on what I had observed about her during this trip, it was clear that she was fiercely committed to her Jewish faith and culture. Her passion for her people was evident. I wondered what she thought about a woman like myself: chasing the truth across the world to find out about her family.

I don't think I ever answered the question. I feel the connection to the Jewish faith and culture in the sense that it represents who my parents were and it also represents the death of their faith and lives as Jews. If I am Jewish because my mother was Jewish, I take pride in that. I am proud to be the daughter of a woman who survived the Holocaust and all of its tragedy. I am sad that she lived a life of fabricating her faith identity, running from her past, keeping secrets for decades, and fearing persecution.

The trip to Topoľčany will be remembered as the physical embodiment of the journey to find answers about my family. Although there were no records or documents to be found, be-

Abandoned building in Topoľčany, Slovakia (visited by author in 2016)

The road leading to Topoľčany, Slovakia (visited by the author in 2016)

ing in the earthly presence of the town that my dad and his family came from was my first tangible connection to my family history. So much of my research has been through e-mails, phone calls, and letters. Topoľčany is the living, physical reminder of the past.

A Remarkable Find in Vancouver and a Real Link

◇ JUDITH GURFINKEL ◇

SUNNY ISLES BEACH, FLORIDA

FINDING JUDITH was remarkable. It changed my entire understanding of who Aunt Blanche was. Up until I discovered Judith, I held to the story that my parents told me about Blanche; that she had reported or threatened to report Dad to the U.S. government for having connections to the Communist Party. It's not a story that you think your parents would make up because you believe what they tell you. But by now, I had discovered that so many of their stories were fabricated. I say this without judgement; I don't know what it would be like to leave your faith, your family, and your past behind as a way to obliterate the atrocities of the Holocaust.

In 2016, when I discovered that Aunt Blanche died in Florida at the age of 99, I was curious as to who may have been with her at the end of her life. As far as I knew, she had never married again or had children and it troubled me that she may have died alone.

The knowledge of her death made me wonder even more why she vanished from our lives. What if I had lost a chance to know more, and it had been possible to talk to her? There was angst in this discovery, a lost possibility to better understand our family background.

Thinking that I might find information about who may have been with her at the end of her life, I wrote to the State of Florida to request her death certificate. Death certificates contain valuable glimmers of information about a person. Details may vary from state to state and in some instances the cause of death is not available if the death occurred less than fifty years ago. Information on a death certificate may include:

- Birthdate, birthplace, race, and social security number
- State, county, or city of death
- Date of death
- Facility or street address where death occurred
- Decedent's occupation and education; confirmation of whether the individual served in the U.S. armed forces
- Names of decedent's mother and father
- Informant's name, address, and relationship to the decedent (this is the person who provides the data for the death certificate, often a relative).
- Name of the cemetery, crematory, or other place for disposition of the body
- Name of the funeral facility

Each of these pieces of data may be a path to finding more information about someone. The importance of each element is probably different depending on who is doing the research. I was hoping to find out if there was anyone in my aunt's life at the time she died. This discovery, based on information in her death certificate, was a game-changer.

The document arrived on a beautiful, sunny Saturday afternoon. I remember hearing the sound of the lawn mower as I retrieved the mail. As I quickly looked at Blanche's death certificate, I was immediately drawn to the section where the informant was named: Judith Gurfinkel of Vancouver, British Columbia. She was listed as Blanche's daughter. I was stunned. My heart was pounding as I stared at the document. It took a few minutes to catch my breath and look at it again. Someone who knew my aunt.

I ran outside waving the document in my hand to get my husband's attention over the drone of the lawn mower. My thoughts were moving quickly, one after the other, colliding in my head with disbelief that there was someone who knew my aunt. A daughter? As John looked at the document, I spoke rapidly, vocalizing one question after another.

What will this finding uncover? I began to think about the possibilities.

Did Blanche have a child while she was in Europe that she revealed?
Did she hide this child away to be reunited many years later?

Could she have had a child after we no longer had contact with her?
Who was Judith?
Did Mom and Dad ever know her?

Knowing that my family history was shrouded with so many untold secrets, anything was possible.

This was the discovery I was looking for: someone who could tell me more about my family. But what if she doesn't want to talk to me? If she had a relationship with Blanche, what did she know about me, my sister, or our parents?

I held these thoughts for the weekend but realized that actually contacting Judith Gurfinkel was my next step. I thought about how I might communicate with her.

Blanche Donath's death certificate (obtained by author in 2016)

I was at a point in the research where my mind was going in a million directions. My overactive imagination kicked in like a detective trying to solve a mystery. I imagined scenarios about what might be the answer. Many were not realistic or sound. Months of relentless research were opening possibilities I had never imagined. My brain was working in ways that it had never worked before. Every question ended in another question: where do I go to discover what I need to know? Who can I contact or write to? The rush of success that came with every find was addictive and the agony of a dead end pushed me even harder. I desperately wanted more of the truth, which had been withheld for so long.

In my excitement, I wanted to call Judith right away, but as I thought about it, I realized that the call might not be welcome. All I knew was that Judith was listed as Blanche's daughter. I tried to put myself in her shoes. How would I respond to a phone call from someone I didn't know who told me that my name was on a death certificate and announced themselves as niece of the deceased?

I Googled Judith's name and confirmed that she lived in Vancouver. But I needed more, something beyond a name on a death certificate to connect her to Blanche. Once again, disbelief surrounded me and the relentless searching resumed.

I started with a search for real estate records for the address listed on the death certificate: 230-174th Street, Sunny Isles Beach, Florida. In the sale history of the apartment, I found that the unit was sold in February 2006. The sellers were listed as Judith Gurfinkel and the estate of Blanche Donath.

On March 16, 2016, I wrote:

Dear Judith:

My name is Orlene Allen Weyland and I am from Old Saybrook, CT (USA). I am writing to you in the hope that you can help me understand more about my family history related to my paternal aunt Blanche Donath, who was my father's sister.

So that you can understand the context of this letter, I have been researching my family history for the past 15 months through a variety of sources including ancestry.com, yadvashem.org, Jewishishgen.org and a trip to the U.S. Holocaust Memorial Museum in Washington D.C. This included a meeting with their research staff to obtain additional information about my family.

As part of my research, I obtained Blanche's death certificate where your name was cited as the informant related to her death in 2005. Until I began this research project, I did not know that Blanche had left New York to move to Florida. To my knowledge, she and my parents did not have contact after the 1960's or early 1970's.

The information I am seeking is to understand what happened to Blanche's parents (Jakob Adler and Julia Adler, nee Schlesinger) as well as her sister Kamila and her family (whose married name I do not know) and a brother whose name I do not know. Her brother, L. Larry Allen M.D., formerly Ladislav Adler, was my father. He left Czechoslovakia after graduating from Medical School in Bratislava and was then in the British Army before he came to the United States. I don't know the specific circumstances or how my father was able to get out of the country at that time. He practiced medicine here in the U.S. both in private practice in Long Island, NY and enjoyed a long career with the Veteran's Administration. He passed away in 1989 in New York City.

I would be grateful for an opportunity to talk with you to hear more about my aunt and any information you can share. I am hoping you are open to having a phone call with me (given the time difference in our locations, maybe we could schedule a time), or if we can communicate through e-mail, please let me know what would be convenient for you.

My husband and I will be in Prague in April and may have the opportunity to go to Topoľčany, where the Adler family lived. Any additional information I can obtain would be so helpful in making this trip.

I mailed the letter with a return receipt request and waited. Every day I tracked the letter through the USPS website; the more I thought about the possibility of talking to Judith, the more excited I became. I tried to prepare myself for the possibility that she might not respond or be open to a conversation.

About two weeks later (it really took that long for the letter to arrive in Vancouver), my telephone rang. When I looked at the caller ID, it had a British Columbia location displayed. My heart was in my throat and my hands were shaking when I picked up the phone. What I heard was a slightly tentative, but warm and welcoming voice 3,000 miles away. The relief in getting this call was astounding. All I could say was, "Judith, I can't believe you called." I was overwhelmed. This was the first time I had spoken to someone who was a living connection to my family.

We shared our respective relationships with Blanche. Within a few minutes, I knew that Judith was Blanche's stepdaughter; Tony was Judith's father, the boyfriend from Blanche's earlier life.

Judith knew that Blanche had a brother who was a doctor but had no idea that my sister and I existed. She commented that Blanche was hesitant to talk about her relationship with him and was vague in her comments. She told Judith that, "he was busy." The vagueness of this was stirring something inside me; I could never imagine my dad being "too busy" for his own sister. I kept the thought to myself for later discussion.

She said that Blanche had been in communication with her sister Kamila, who remained in Europe and died in about 1990. She lived in Bratislava with her husband and son, Peter, before Peter died.

Judith spoke with love and affection for Blanche. She felt Blanche to be a wonderful person who lived a very happy life with Judith's father, Tony Binetter. She knew Blanche for over forty years and shared that she and her children had wonderful memories of the times they spent with Blanche and her father. He had passed away a few years before.

How sweet to learn that Blanche experienced the love of a

man, his children, and grandchildren. But also how sad that neither my sister nor I had the possibility of that experience with Blanche.

Judith met Blanche during one of her trips to Israel around 1969, several years after Blanche and Tony met. They moved to Florida in 1986 when Tony retired and lived a good, relaxed life. Both were healthy and able until their very latest years. She also said that Blanche never spoke about her experiences in Europe during the war. Judith remembered that her daughter observed the tattoo on Blanche's arm; the permanent imprint of the Holocaust. This too, was never discussed by Blanche. Judith's sense was that her father knew of Blanche's experiences in Europe, but did not speak of them either.

Judith told me that after Blanche's death, she found a box in the apartment in Florida that contained documents and pictures, as she described them, of people she did not know. She thought some of them may have been pictures of me and my sister, as well as our parents.

The contents of the box Judith spoke about would have been cumbersome to send. They also deserved an in-person discovery. She did, however, e-mail several pictures; one of Blanche with Judith and her two children. The smile on Blanche's face in that picture could have lit up a room. The other picture of our Aunt Kamila and her husband at the graveside of their son, Peter, was a haunting reflection of grief and pain.

Along with these pictures, Judith also wrote a letter following our phone call.

On April 1, 2016 she wrote:

Dear Orlene,

Thank you so much for your letter and the initiative you took to investigate about Blanche. I am very happy for her that you, as her closest relative, finally connect with her and her memory.

I tried to summarize the information I collected from looking into the box of photos Blanche kept and few other documents I found in files from the

Miami apartment. I may have more just need to do a thorough search. I would very much like to give you all or most of the documents and photos you find relevant, in person or by mail.

Photos I found are probably of your grandparents, Blanche herself from times before she came to the US, her husband (Donath), her brother (your father) and many photos of Kamila and her son Peter. There is a photo of the grave of Ella Adler (born November 27, 1904 and died July 30, 1940), maybe you know who she is. I also have later photos of Blanche with my father on vacations and with friends.

Blanche's sister, Kamila Pavlanska, lived in Bratislava at 2 Budovatelska Street. But there are photos with Peter from other, probably vacation places. Peter was born in 1946 and died on October 9, 1958, don't have any information in what circumstances. Kamila died ca. 1990.

Blanche arrived to New York aboard the Queen Mary on January 18, 1951 and nationalized in 1958. She worked as seamstress at B. Altman & Co., Lord & Taylor, maybe other fashion houses and was a member of ILGWU, International Ladies' Garment Workers' Union.

I got to know Blanche for the first time in Israel around 1969. I think, she and my father, Anthony Binetter, met sometime in 1966 or 1967 and lived together since in Brooklyn. Later they visited Israel 3 or 4 times until they moved to Miami in 1986, when my father retired.

In Florida they had a small apartment in Sunny Isles (North Miami Beach) and lived a good relaxed life. I visited them many times with my husband and children or on my own. They were both healthy and able until the very last year before they died. Blanche had a hip fracture in 1998 and was not very active after that but mentally still fine. My father died in 2002.

My paternal grandmother was also an Adler, Ilonka Binetter (Adler) born 1886 in Topoľčany, Nitria

Region, Slovakia and died 1976 in Belgium. She was the daughter of Dr. Armin Adler and Judit Adler (Lowinger). Dr. Armin Adler was born ca. 1851 in Topoľčany, Nitra Region, Slovakia and died on May 31, 1905. His siblings were Simon Adler, Jakab Adler and Fani Rosenthal (Adler). It always puzzled me why Blanche and my father never investigated their origin and the possibility of being related. Although Adler is a very common name but Tapolcany is small enough…. It could be interesting to find out something in your research.

I knew Blanche for 40 years and there are many other details I can tell you about her life, but only the years she has been with my father. She rarely mentioned her previous life and definitely nothing about her life during the war. My children and I have wonderful memories from the times we spent with my father and Blanche. I am attaching a photo of Blanche with us, probably from 1982.

If you have questions, please call or e-mail and I will be happy to share any information I have.

Sincerely,
Judith Gurfinkel

I knew I had to go to Vancouver to meet Judith, the only living person who had a long-term relationship with someone in my family. My sister and I discussed it and decided we would go together, so we arranged to meet in Minneapolis in the fall of 2016. I'd leave from Connecticut, Susie from Maryland. We'd fly to Vancouver together.

And what a trip it was!

We met Judith later that day and my heart was filled with instant affection for her. Judith is a petite, dark-haired woman with soft and expressive eyes. Her smile lights up a room and her enthusiasm is contagious. I discovered very quickly that Judith is an intuitive woman who can read a situation or relationship with great accuracy. Her perspectives are thoughtful and kind.

We started our relationship sharing information about our respective families interspersed with snippets of the research.

Judith told us about her daughter who lives in Israel and her son who lives close by in Vancouver. We shared the love of being grandmothers; Judith and I each have three grandchildren.

Top: Author's sister Susie, Judith Garfinkel , the author, and Judith's husband Michael 2016 in Vancouver where they all first met.
Bottom: Blanche (center) with Judith (left) and her two children - courtesy of Judith Garfinkel, circa 1982

My sister had just become a grandmother for the first time in 2015. This was a wonderful, soft entrée into getting to know each other. I didn't want to rush into the research and the detail and risk doing all the talking. It was enough to sit and listen to Judith and get a sense of who she was.

She spoke lovingly of Blanche and her relationship with her. We heard a completely different version of her than the one Susie and I had heard in the past from Mom and Dad. This only raised more questions about Blanche's relationship with them. How could a woman who is so loved be the same one who threatened to report Dad to the U.S. Government as being connected to the Communist Party? Understanding that their worlds were strikingly different at that time, it still raised the question. What else could have happened for their relationship to be cut off? Especially when so many in their family had perished?

That evening, we went to dinner with Judith and her lovely husband Michael in Granville Island, a beautiful section of Vancouver. I felt like I had known them forever.

Later in the week, we had the opportunity to meet Judith's son Aran in a coffee house in downtown Vancouver. Susie and I sat across the table from Judith and her son. A vivid memory is Judith asking her Aran if either I or my sister reminded him of Blanche. I fully expected him to say that my sister resembled her most, especially since they shared the same olive skin and dark eyes, just like my dad. To my surprise, he pointed at me. I wish I knew what he saw. If you looked at a picture of me and Blanche you would never see a resemblance. I look more like my mom. Judith thoughtfully observed and shared that I move my hands in the same way Blanche did. Wow. Some things really are inherited.

Susie and I went to Judith's home and spent hours poring over the pictures and documents she had discovered in Blanche's apartment after her death. We talked about each picture in great detail; it was the first time we had seen a picture of Zoltan, Blanche's first husband who perished in the Holocaust.

We discovered pictures of Julia and Jakob Adler, our grandparents, who also perished at the hands of the Nazis. Pictures of Susie and me as little girls when we lived in Washington,

The author's Aunt Kamila and her husband at their son's grave (discovered in Blanche's apartment after her death). Courtesy of Judith Gurfinkel.

D.C. Pictures of other people we didn't know; maybe friends of Blanche's or relatives we didn't know. Documents that described Blanche's medical condition following her emigration to the U.S. She had applied for restitution from the German government and as part of the process underwent a complete physical/mental evaluation. As I read the translations weeks later (thanks to a dear friend of my sister's), I was horrified to see in words, the treatment that Blanche experienced in four camps from 1944 through her liberation in 1945.

We also found Blanche's papers from her marriage to Zoltan. What a beautiful couple they made. Now there was a face to his name; he too, was murdered by the Nazis.

One picture in particular will probably haunt me forever; a picture of Kamila and her husband at Peter's grave.

◊

Another mystery in the puzzle is a picture we found of the gravesite of Ella Adler. Born in 1904, she died in 1940. Judith had no information as to who she was or why Blanche had kept this picture. Of course, this raised more questions. Could she have been the wife of the Adler brother whose name we do not

know, the one described by our dad as having died in the war?
We may never know the answer to these questions despite the
exhaustive search for any other information about Ella Adler. I
use the word "may" so as not to close the door on future research.

◇

Judith guided us through the pictures and documents and
translated as well. Every time we saw a picture or document, I
could feel the anguish welling up inside. It felt strangely out of
context to see documents and pictures of myself, my sister, my
parents, and other family members that were found in a box by
someone I didn't know.

◇

I wondered if Aunt Blanche ever looked at the pictures. Why did
she keep them? Even before she approached my sister in 1973
at Bloomingdale's, had she thought of contacting us? Even after
that, when mom prohibited any contact with her, did Blanche
want to have a relationship with Susie and me? Why had she
not told Judith about us?

◇

Susie and I were poring through the pictures when we found
one of Dad when he was a young boy. Never having seen a
picture of him at such a young age, we looked at each other
in wide-eyed disbelief. It was like looking at a picture of my
youngest grandchild, Weyland, who was four at the time. When
you put the pictures side by side, the resemblance is uncanny.

What I see in that picture is how blessed my grandson is. Not
to have to face the traumas and decisions that my dad did. Not to
have his family murdered at the hands of the Nazis. Not to have
to flee his native country and leave his family behind. Not to
have to give up his faith and run from demons. So, he is blessed.

One of the documents we found was a Hanukkah card from
a woman named Trudi whose return address was in Queens,
New York. Judith knew about Trudi, as she and Blanche had
worked together in the garment district in New York. She also
mentioned that Trudi was the only person for her to call when
Blanche died in 2005. Judith resonated with such sadness about
this. There was no one else in Blanche's life outside of Judith's

Ladislav Adler, the author's father (age unknown)
and the author's grandson, Weyland Smith

family who had loved her as their own. Although Blanche passed away six years after dad, I wonder if she would have wanted to know about his death. There was no one to tell her. They both died on July 29th. I wonder if that's a coincidence.

Through some online searching I found Trudi and crossed-matched information from multiple sources to be sure I had found the right person.

I wrote her a letter and asked her to call me if she was open to talking about Blanche. My sister and I also decided that it would be good to meet her as well even if she didn't have any information. We were more interested in hearing about her relationship with Blanche. One more person who might help us understand who Blanche was.

Just like Judith, Trudi called me when she received the letter; she didn't have much more to share but was open to meeting my sister and me. She had, in fact, worked with Blanche in the garment industry and it sounded as though they were good friends.

In March of 2017, Susie and I met in Manhattan with a plan to see Trudi the next afternoon. We hired a car service to get us to Trudi's home in Queens; it was a stone's throw to where I used to live, so the neighborhood looked familiar.

What lovely hosts she and her husband were. They welcomed us into their home as though they had known us for a long time. It looked as though Trudi had been cooking and baking for hours. Over lunch, we talked about Blanche. Trudi shared that she had not spoken very much about her life in Europe. Trudi and her husband had visited with Blanche and Tony when they lived in Brooklyn; it sounded as though they got together socially on a somewhat regular basis. They shared their own family pictures with us as well, describing each one in great detail; weddings, grandchildren, and holidays.

Trudi described the work she and Blanche did in the New York fashion world. They made sample dresses for the top designers of the industry. Blanche had been a seamstress at B. Altman and Co., Lord & Taylor and was a member of the ILGWU, International Ladies' Garment Workers Union.

My sister was particularly engaged by this. She had a stellar career with Bloomingdale's in merchandising and buying for the store, and it was in Bloomingdale's that Blanche found her so many years later and posed the idea of them getting together.

Susie had an interesting idea as to how Blanche may have discovered her in Bloomingdale's in 1973. My first wedding dress came from Lord and Taylor, where Blanche had worked (we don't know the dates). Susie wondered if Blanche had seen our family name on the alteration instructions on the wedding dress and since I have an unusual first name, she thought it possible that Blanche made that connection. Could she have recognized our family and discovered that Susie worked at Bloomingdales? Given Blanche's history and longevity and likely connections in the garment industry, it's possible that she found Susie this way. This is another example of how family research raises questions and possibilities. Even if there is not a way to confirm anything, it stretches the imagination to keep asking questions.

Susie and Blanche shared the same talents and I think this was a very personal connection for her with Blanche. My sister can sew or create anything with fabric; she used to make Barbie dresses for our dolls with a little sewing machine. Later she made dresses, including her prom dress, and was a regular designer of my daughter's Halloween costumes. By comparison my ability to sew even a button is limited at best.

We left Trudi's a few hours later, complete with bread and treats that she insisted we take. Although we didn't gain much information, it was another avenue to pursue in the research. They don't all end with information, but meeting someone who knew our aunt was another gift to be appreciated in this process.

◊

As I think about the documents and pictures in that box, I still wonder why Blanche kept them and yet revealed so little to Judith about her past or her family. Did she feel it best to "let sleeping dogs lie," as mom used to say? Did she take my dad's perspective of, "don't look back?" How can a family be torn apart like this, especially when they seemed close at one time?

◊

Top: Blanche Donath and Tony Binetter with Judith's son.
Bottom: Blanche and Tony's gravesite in Hollywood, Florida, visited by the
author's sister in 2018.

Visits from Mom and Dad

I STARTED experiencing visits from Mom and Dad in 1998. The first time it happened, I was home alone baking cookies for the holidays, listening to Christmas music and admiring my beautiful tree. I love Christmas trees and holiday lights; the glow of the lights and the colorful sparkle of a vast collection of ornaments evokes a sense of peace and happiness.

This love of light also translates to every other area of my surroundings at home. I love different aspects of light; the brilliant sunshine in my kitchen at mid-day, lighting up the stained-glass on one side of the room. The early rays that come through the shutters in the bedroom, beckoning me to welcome the day. I also love the evening light of the fireplace in our cozy living room. The dark is welcome at the end of a winter day; I feel wrapped in the arms of my home in its warmth and character.

My attention to the light is a conscious response to my environment. Each ray or cloud provides movement of the light. It's late afternoon as I write this and the winter sun is beginning to fade. Soon it will be time to turn on the lamp in my office, a ceramic lamp with bright flowers of red, blue, and gold on the base and a red shade that softens the room. A different kind of light from the sun, but equally as centering.

When this first visit came, I was centered with the lights from my Christmas tree and the warm glow of the fireplace. I felt my parent's presence, not a physical presence but something different. I was also doing the things that make me happy.

I began talking to them aloud, as though we were on the phone and I was catching them up on my day-to-day life. Nothing significant, just letting them know how Bonnie (my daughter) was doing, what I had been up to. This went on for about twenty minutes. Between the words, I was tearing up, but I kept talking. And as fast as the visit started, it ended. It was powerful and exhausting and I wanted them to come back. I tried several times in the following weeks to summon them; in retrospect it sounds silly to me.

The "visits," and I've had more since then, are unpredictable. They come in different settings; I've had visits at home, when I'm walking by the water where I live, during a church service, when I'm baking (I wonder about the significance of that - my dad loved everything I baked for him). There was nothing I could do to make a visit happen just by asking for it, though.

One visit that really strikes me is when I started doing research on my family. It was in 2015, right after I discovered that my grandfather, Oskar Brahm had been deported and murdered by the Nazis. On top of the shock and grief that came with this discovery was a sense of disloyalty to my parents. After all, they did everything they could to hide this secret; their need was for me and my sister to never know. I felt that I had betrayed them.

The guilt and conflict about this were central in my discussion with them that day. I was walking in my neighborhood and about to cross over the causeway which crosses the Long Island Sound and connects my neighborhood with the Borough of Fenwick here in Old Saybrook. I love this walk; the water in the sound looks different every time I cross the causeway. This particular day, it was still cold out and there were no boats to be seen. As I watched the sun shine and dance across the water, I felt my parent's presence.

I think I had been waiting for this visit to talk to them about feeling some guilt and conflict in unearthing their secrets. I asked them to understand why I was doing this. That I wanted my daughter and my three grandchildren, my sister's children and two grandchildren, to understand who their family is. To never forget their experiences as people who were persecuted because of who they were.

It was also important for me to tell them that I understood why they never disclosed their true pasts. I wasn't angry with them but flooded with love and compassion, for what it was like for them to destroy their past as a way to protect us. The energy it took to live this secret must have been exhausting. The fear of persecution or discovery could have been debilitating, and yet they carried on, never revealing the truth.

The visits seem to be getting further and further apart but have been significant for me. I wonder if the change in frequency is connected to the research I've been doing about my family and the soul searching around faith. Is it possible that my parents' spirits are at greater peace and are reconciled to the truth being out? Is it coincidence that the first visit in 1998 came the same year I visited a Rabbi to confirm that my parents were Jewish?

436 Shalom to You Now

Sha - lom to you now, sha - lom, my friend

May God's full mer - cies bless you, my friends
be with

In all your liv - ing and through your lov - ing
through all

Christ be your sha - lom, Christ be your sha - lom.

WORDS: Elise S. Eslinger, 1980
MUSIC: Traditional Spanish melody; harm. Carlton R. Young, 1989

Words © 1983, harm. © 1989, The United Methodist Publishing House

SOMOS DEL S

♩=1

Alt. setting

Shalom to You Now

THE PATH to looking at my faith has been no small venture. There are always more questions than answers.

What I am about to say should not be misunderstood; my path to faith is a late experience for me and religion was never a central focus for our family. My religious education and church attendance ended in the late 1960s. Mom and Dad felt that it was up to me and my sister to decide how much or how little we wanted to pursue religion. I chose not to participate and tossed religion aside. By then, Mom and Dad had ceased to attend church on any regular basis. I became less and less of a believer in anything. I could hear my dad's comments in my head about Jesus not being the Son of God; I could hear the literal messages about resurrection and miracle birth and tossed them to the wind. If I attended a church for a wedding or funeral, I stopped singing hymns or reciting the Lord's Prayer. Out of respect, I stood and sat as part of the church protocol, but that was about it for me. I had become the living translation of my father.

When I married for the first time in 1973, it was in a Presbyterian church on Queens Boulevard in Elmhurst, New York, officiated by our childhood minister and close family friend, Reverend Dr. Paul Ludwig. He traveled from Pennsylvania to perform the ceremony. Dr. Ludwig and his wife were two of my parents' closest friends; in fact, they were designated to be our guardians if anything had ever happened to Mom and Dad when we were growing up. I wanted Dr. Ludwig to officiate based on the long and close relationship our family had with his. I probably would have been married by a J.P. if he had not been able to do this.

Beyond getting married in a church, I didn't attend services or give much thought to anything related to religious or spiritual growth. When my daughter was born in 1980, we decided not to baptize her. I felt it to be hypocritical to engage in this ritual with no commitment to the faith. Her father agreed. A lapsed Catholic, he had no objections. I discovered a few years later that my former mother-in-law performed her own baptism in her home because she was worried that my daughter would go to hell if she wasn't baptized or christened. My former mother-in-law was a devout Catholic and as angry as I was about what she had done, no real harm was caused. She was acting in what she thought was my daughter's best interest.

As I was raising Bonnie, I thought long and hard about how to explain the holidays we celebrated. Christmas is the more obvious and tangible one; aside from the grossly over-commercialized aspect of this holiday, it is recognized as the day that Christ was born. It wasn't difficult to explain that this was the day we celebrated the birth of a visionary man.

Easter was the harder one. Most sacred of all Christian holidays, I understood the crucifixion and resurrection. I bought into some of the secular observation of this holiday, the Easter Bunny and chocolate but adamantly refused to have my daughter sit in the Easter Bunny's lap at the mall. The idea of sitting on the lap of a giant bunny with big, pink eyes and enormous ears was just too creepy.

I came to an understanding for myself, that Easter was a time of hope and rebirth. Christ was murdered because of who he was and what he taught; this is a long-standing truth for me. Resurrection, as I explained to my daughter, is connected to rebirth and hope. I still feel that way. You can call it resurrection if you prefer, but the meaning for me is rebirth. Not just physical rebirth as we experience in our gardens, but an opportunity to grow a little brighter and more colorful.

For most of my adult life, I pursued little in terms of religious or spiritual exploration. I got myself stuck in a rather narrow view of religion; I didn't see it as a path to growth but rather an organized ritual for people to follow one day a week. I remember Dad saying that so many churchgoers were hypocrites, smiling and being nice on Sundays and not living the words for the rest of the week. He felt strongly that going to church was a crutch. His cynicism strikes me as a way of saying that his faith and his God had failed him. His words still ring in my head but I continue to evolve. It's a work in progress.

Years later, on Christmas Eve of 2007, I decided to go to church for the early evening service. I can't describe the "why"; only that I had been feeling a need to begin to explore something bigger than myself and thought church might be a good start. I had not attended church services on any regular basis since my early teens. So, at 55 years old, when the spirit moved me, I moved with it. What was the worst that could happen?

This was the time for me to bring this need to a more conscious level and do something besides think about it and call myself "spiritual" with no basis or foundation to go on. Maybe it had to do with becoming a grandmother for the first time in August of that year. Seeing my only daughter hold her firstborn and take in the loving softness of her eyes and face when she gazed at that beautiful baby triggered a level of joy that crept into other areas of my life. Becoming a grandmother pulled my heart into a different and softer place and the need to experience joy at a different level became evident. Something had opened up that I really couldn't describe.

I picked the First Church of Christ (Congregational) Church in Wethersfield, close to where I lived. As a lover of Christmas music, particularly the traditional hymns, I thought this would be a good start. When I walked into the church, the sight took my breath away. The sanctuary was decorated with rows and rows of brilliant red poinsettias and, against the candle lit chandeliers and evening lighting, the effect was magical. I picked an end seat in a back pew just in case I needed to make a fast escape. The church experience was a new exploration and I wasn't sure how comfortable this would be. It was also a way to avoid interaction with people in the church. I wasn't ready for conversation or any involvement.

When the music started, I instantly felt it inside and the tears rolled. It was grief, sadness, and a longing to connect to something bigger than myself. But tears and feelings of sadness accompanied by organ music are not a new experience for me. This has been happening to me for as long as I can remember, when I hear organ music at a wedding, funeral, in a church, or the music at a bar mitzvah ceremony. It also happens when I hear the National Anthem. I still cry on the 4th of July. My mom and dad loved all of the American patriotic music. It's no coincidence that I love the 4th of July as they celebrated their wedding anniversary, and their pride in being naturalized American citizens, on July 5th. I often wonder if it's also no coincidence that my grandson was born on July 4th. A well-timed gift from their spirits?

Just before my daughter's wedding in 2001, I listened to the music she and her fiancé had picked for their ceremony enough times to cry and get it out of my system before their wedding day. I still cry when I hear Pachelbel's Canon in D in any venue. It's a beautiful memory.

I attended this church for about a year and began to look forward to the weekly service, message, and music. I felt connected to something inside; I could feel a door opening ever so slightly and was beginning to get a little glimpse of light. My heart was beginning to open up to look at my faith with all my questions and doubts. When the choir sang, I could hear Mom singing along beside me. The music filled me with joy and sadness and provided a wonderful outlet for bringing the memories to life. Every time I left that church, I felt a relief, or release from the tangle inside. Even with my questions and doubts, I began to look at the church experience as a way to reflect and get centered. I continued to sit in the back of the church. I still wasn't ready to engage in the after-church social scene and discovered that this was a meaningful way for me to be alone in my thoughts and reflections. It was uplifting to really understand my need for this and shape it in the way that felt most comfortable. That's a long way from where I had been earlier in my adult life, rejecting all forms of a faith relationship.

About two years later and early in my relationship with John, my now-husband, I attended worship services at the North Madison Congregational Church, in Madison, Connecticut. John has been actively involved in this congregation over a number of years, interrupted by his moves around the country and to Europe. He is a man of faith; he has taken the leap to believe in something bigger than himself and lives the words of the prophet Jesus in his actions, deeds, and contributions.

It's a small church with a congregation of about two hundred people. The sanctuary is pristine and simple, and is at its most beautiful in the morning when sunlight is coming through the shuttered windows. We used to sit in the third or fourth row on the left side facing the front of the church. We both love feeling the warmth on our backs as the rays come through the shutters. Since then, we alternate where we sit as a way of getting a different view of the choir and to sit near different friends in the congregation. I also love this church because it's not air-conditioned in the summer. The soft warm breezes that flow through the sanctuary add just one more dimension to the experience of reflection and getting centered.

The first time I attended this church with John I was apprehensive, despite his assurances that this was a wonderful and welcoming group of people. I had not yet met his friends from the church, but quickly found that my fears were unfounded. If I had to describe the definition of "welcoming," this group would be just that. I was taken in like an old friend, naturally with curiosity about who I was and how John and I met.

I got hooked that day and, of course, it had to do with music. This congregation ends every service with the "Shalom" hymn accompanied by Linda Juliani, one of the most gifted organists I have ever heard. Linda is a petite, blue-eyed, silver-haired woman with a smile that lights up a room. She is also one of the people who welcomed me in with open arms. I could listen to her play the organ all day long; what a gift she has.

When I first heard "Shalom" the tears came from nowhere and as I sang this beautiful hymn, my eyes caught sight of the large, bare wooden cross that hangs in the front of the sanctuary. I couldn't move my eyes away from it. And the more I looked, the more I cried. At that time, I had no knowledge of how so many in my family perished during the Holocaust, but believe this was my history beckoning to me through song and the physical symbol of sacrifice.

This was nine years ago and to this day, I still weep when I hear and sing this hymn. The words and music resonate with something that fills me with sadness and joy.

The joy comes from my 2011 wedding ceremony. John and I used "Shalom" to end our ceremony and asked our respective families to sing with us, led by my niece, Julia Pitcher Worcester who clearly inherited my mom's gift of voice. What I love about this is that when I hear "Shalom" in church, it brings me back to our beautiful wedding, so the joy is even more intense when I sing and, ultimately, cry.

The sadness comes from knowing the harsh truth of my family history. The significance of that cross in its starkness in terms of sacrifice and cruelty keeps me from being able to look away, especially knowing how so many in my family perished in the Holocaust. I shed tears for my mom and dad who lived to deny and hide their true past. I shed tears for my Aunt Blanche, who survived the horrifying experience of being in four concentration camps. I shed tears for the family I never knew who perished at the hands of the Nazis; my grandfather, Oskar Brahm, my grandparents Jakub and Julia Adler, my uncle Zoltan Donath and the seven million people who were brutally murdered because of who they were.

For me, the hymns and music are a path to reflection and glimpses of clarity. They open up something that persuades me to move away from my head and to my heart. Some are familiar to me in music and words and are clear and present reminders of my parents, especially Mom. She had a beautiful voice and loved to sing; and she sang often. Not just in church as I remember, but when she was doing her daily rounds of housework. She was a fanatic cleaner and I remember her pushing the carpet sweeper around singing "Summertime" from the musical "Porgy and Bess." She had a voice similar to Roberta Flack. Lucky for us, my niece was the chosen recipient for this particular gift.

When I hear these hymns today, I feel as though my mom is standing next to me singing along so smoothly and naturally. And I can attest that you can't sing and cry at the same time. This is a frequent experience for me and I am fortunate to now belong to a church community that embraces whatever you need to do during the service. They actually refer to me affectionately as the "sobbing section."

Since I attended and had been baptized in the Presbyterian Church (and quite frankly I know little about the history of this denomination) and hearing the words of God in Sunday School, it is no small thing to hear that Jesus is not the Son of God and that there is no such thing as resurrection. These are the tenets that strike the hardest in terms of the ideological differences I heard as a child and that I continue to struggle with as an adult.

Do I believe that Jesus was the Son of God? Why do I feel outright resistance when I hear those words? Why am I so much more comfortable with the perspective that he was a prophet, a teacher, and visionary? And yet I take from church services the ideas and thinking that resonate and leave the rest behind. It's rare when I leave a service and don't feel uplifted.

I've spent many hours in thought and in discussion with my husband, who offers no judgement about my feelings but offers encouragement to ask questions and acknowledge my doubts. I spent some time with the minister who married us to talk with him about my doubts and feeling torn in two directions with no sign of reconciliation between the two.

Dr. Jay, as we call him, is a liberal, non-judgmental pastor whose counsel focuses on freeing my logical mind from the literal messages of the church and integrating the teachings of Christ as a life standard. Dr. Jay is a tall, bearded man with a soft and approachable style. His own life events are not dissimilar to what so many of us experience; marriage, divorce, children, substance abuse issues in a family, parenting adult children. Dr. Jay is also someone who championed a movement within the church to become what is known as Open and Affirming. This is a public covenant taken by a church congregation to welcome, love, and include persons of every sexual orientation, gender identity, and gender expression. No small feat, even in a liberal congregation.

Having heard Dad eschew the literal messages and stories taught in Christianity, my understanding of his thinking has changed. He said what was on his mind with few filters. Even with what we might describe as a cynicism around religion, I think what he meant was that the literal stories are not the important lessons. This thinking played out in his opinion and judgement of the Jewish rite of bar mitzvah; how many times did I hear him say that a thirteen-year-old boy is not a man? His objection to the literal was consistent across both faith perspectives. I wish he had talked more about all of this. But it's probably time for me to let all of that go and stay focused on the teachings. Maybe that's the real path.

Another pastor and advisor, Reverend Jim Latimer, has played a major role in my spiritual development. His first career was in engineering and his path took him to the ministry and pastoral coaching. I first met Jim in 2013, when he joined the North Madison Congregational Church as the settled pastor. Jim is a trim, athletic looking man with the healthy facial sheen of someone who is physically active. His speaking style is articulate and clearly demonstrates the amount of research and reading he does in preparing a sermon. He opens every service with: "No matter who you are or where you are in your life journey, you are welcome here." He poses questions throughout his sermons and welcomes comments and responses from his congregation. I came to appreciate Jim as a brilliant intellectual and spiritual advisor. In his role as minister, Jim poses conceptual frameworks that bring real life issues to the table.

He also has a wonderful and affirming message about spiritual development, which takes into account where you are in the continuum. When he spoke about this a few years ago, I walked away thinking that I was (and still am) in the right place: continuing to listen, to question, to challenge and be challenged. I can't count the number of times I listened to Jim, all the while thinking, "is he talking to me directly?" or "did he write that just for me?" Jim also has the unique gift of being a true "performer" in front of a congregation. Although an introvert by style, he moves around and engages response during a sermon, asks questions and poses possibilities. Jim has a way of shifting the paradigm. During one discussion in which we were talking about some of the literal stories heard in the Bible and how difficult they are to understand; he posed the idea that we could focus more on what the writer or author was trying to convey. For me, this was a game changer; it helped me through my continuing conflict with literal vs. spiritual. Very liberating.

I was recently asked to read the introduction to the congregation at a weekly church service. As I prepared for this, I was struck with how this particularly resonated with what I heard at home when I was growing up. Even if you take out any reference to the Bible or the author, it still stands in terms of the value system I was raised in.

The message from Matthew's Gospel is the third of three chapters that we call "Jesus' Sermon on the Mount." The big question in these words is simple: how do we treat other people once we have become followers of Jesus? Jesus' audience has experienced the ways of pious scholars and teachers, and it has seemed to them like those who claim to know the holy truth turn around and use it against other people (I can hear my dad). The values that Jesus offers are different: they require us to take on humility, patience, and tolerance for others.

The Gospel according to Matthew, Chapter 7, verses 1-14:

1. "Don't pick on people, jump on their failures, criticize their faults—unless, of course, you want the same treatment.

2. That critical spirit has a way of boomeranging.

3. It's easy to see a smudge on your neighbor's face and be oblivious to the ugly sneer on your own.

4. Do you have the nerve to say, 'Let me wash your face for you,' when your own face is distorted by contempt?

5. It's this whole traveling road-show mentality all over again, playing a holier-than-thou part instead of just living your part. Wipe that ugly sneer off your own face, and you might be fit to offer a washcloth to your neighbor.

6. "Don't be flip with the sacred. Banter and silliness give no honor to God. Don't reduce holy mysteries to slogans. In trying to be relevant, you're only being cute and inviting sacrilege.

7. "Don't bargain with God. Be direct. Ask for what you need.

8. This isn't a cat-and-mouse, hide-and-seek game we're in.

9. If your child asks for bread, do you trick him with sawdust?

10. If he asks for fish, do you scare him with a live snake on his plate?

11. As bad as you are, you wouldn't think of such a thing. You're at least decent to your own children. So, don't you think the God who conceived you in love will be even better?

12. "Here is a simple, rule-of-thumb guide for behavior: Ask yourself what you want people to do for you, then grab the initia-

tive and do it for them. Add up God's Law and Prophets and this is what you get.

13. "Don't look for shortcuts to God. The market is flooded with surefire, easygoing formulas for a successful life that can be practiced in your spare time. Don't fall for that stuff, even though crowds of people do.

14. The way to life-to God!-is vigorous and requires total attention.

... and from Chapter 7 verses 24-29, The Message Translation

24. "These words I speak to you are not incidental additions to your life, homeowner improvements to your standard of living. They are foundational words, words to build a life on. If you work these words into your life, you are like a smart carpenter who built his house on solid rock.

25. Rain poured down, the river flooded, a tornado hit—but nothing moved that house. It was fixed to the rock.

26. "But if you just use my words in Bible studies and don't work them into your life, you are like a stupid carpenter who built his house on the sandy beach.

27. When a storm rolled in and the waves came up, it collapsed like a house of cards."

28. When Jesus concluded his address, the crowd burst into applause. They had never heard teaching like this.

29. It was apparent that he was living everything he was saying—quite a contrast to their religion teachers! This was the best teaching they had ever heard.

This message helps me reconcile some of the stark differences in what I heard at home and what I was taught in church. It is truly the foundation of my parents' thinking and belief system. This is what resonates in my heart. And it really doesn't matter to me who wrote it or in what literature it resides in.

I believe that the things we do happen for a reason. Sometimes we have to move with the spirit of something even when we don't know why.

There is No Ending

THE EXPERIENCE of discovery and research findings has been an emotional roller coaster. The rush of finding information, the gripping pain of exhuming the stories of my family, the grief for people I never knew, and the sadness in knowing that Mom and Dad spent most of their adult lives bearing these secrets, hiding their past, and denying who they were.

As I write, I still have questions that may not be answered.

The question of why Aunt Blanche and my parents severed their relationship sometime in the early to mid-1960s.

Did Blanche really threaten to report them to the government as being connected to the Communist party? I will never know if there is truth to this statement.

In the conversations I have had with Judith and in light of her glowing description of her relationship with Blanche, she has shed some possible light on the "why." Blanche was evaluated by a physician in 1965 as part of the process for restitution from the German government. It is my understanding, through Judith, that a significant amount of documentation was required to enter this process, which may have included attestation from my dad. If he had refused to assist (we can only speculate that he would not have wanted to publicly identify himself as being Jewish or become involved with anything connected to the German government), it would make sense that their relationship may have been severed. If I try to imagine Blanche asking him for his help and being refused, I can understand that their relationship could have been tested to an impossible limit. Some families sever relationships over disappointments that in comparison, seem much less significant. I'm not judging my aunt, or my dad, this is just a possibility to consider. And we'll never know the answer.

And like the research, one question leads to another. How did my dad come to grips with the knowledge of what became of his family after he left Czechoslovakia in 1939? In his words, he "escaped," so he must have had knowledge of what might be coming. Others I have talked to during the course of the research speculate that his family may have been able to help him get out of the country. As the youngest male child and a physician, it's possible that his family found a way to spare him from the worst. Our family has also wondered if he was assisted in his escape in exchange for information he may have had about the activities in his country.

I wonder what longer term effects this may have held for him. How did he hold on to the knowledge and memory of the fate of his family? How does a person attempt to put something like that behind them? When did he learn the fate of his parents and brother-in-law? When did he learn that Blanche survived four concentration camps?

Maybe there is a side of my dad that I never knew. Maybe I don't fully understand the desperation to survive in a world where being deported, transported, tortured, and gassed to death are a reality. I wish that he had been able to talk about all of this, but my wish may be another glimpse of my limited understanding of his experience and that of his family. I could spend the rest of my life asking these questions to no avail.

I'm saddened every time I think about these questions. Even as I write them, I feel anguish of now knowing the horror my dad may have faced in leaving his family behind. I also feel anguish in knowing that my Aunt Blanche suffered as no human being should ever suffer. I feel as well the horror of knowing that my grandparents and others were brutally murdered.

I still have questions about my mother and her discovery that her step-mother was not her birth mother. It is still painful to have knowledge that she was treated cruelly and abusively. I will never know why Oskar Brahm tolerated this if he knew about it. I may never know if Oskar Brahm was, in fact, my mother's biological father. I will hold that for future research.

I wonder what it was like for her, searching for her father's face in large crowds, hoping and wishing to see him again.

And yet, despite all of this, Mom and Dad found happiness with each other and their new lives. They knew how to have fun, how to laugh and how to love. Their ability to survive, to love, to be the family we were, helps to soften the blow of the discoveries of their secrets.

There is also another cushion that has been a constant theme and reminder during this process. Without exception, every person I met during my journey has provided, in their own unique way, a soft landing spot from the harsh truth I faced.

This experience bears witness to the true nature of people I have met. They shine like beacons of light in the universe and have blessed me countless times in a world where witnessing good has become a daily challenge. And for that, I am forever grateful.

Top: The author's parents with her daughter Bonnie, 1981
Bottom: The author's parents with her niece Julia, 1981

A Letter to My Parents

◊ JANUARY 28, 2018 ◊

THE FIRST Public Story at the North Madison Congregational Church, United Church of Christ, Madison, Connecticut

This letter was written by me and shared with the congregation at the North Madison Congregational Church, United Church of Christ, in Madison, Connecticut. This was the first of what I hope will be many opportunities to share my family history in a very public way. In this setting, I have found acceptance, empathy, and understanding in a community of people who come from different faiths and backgrounds. The letter was written as part of the church's wish to have congregants share stories of their backgrounds.

A letter to Mom and Dad:

I write this to you to tell you that I love you and hope you understand my quest to know and understand your story. I've often wondered if you would be upset about all that I have discovered about our Jewish heritage, especially because your plan was for me and Susie to never know about the horrors that you and your families experienced and having made those discoveries, it only helps me better understand how protective your love was for us both.

So I'll start from the beginning. Knowing that you raised us as Christians, your message to us was to live as Jesus did in terms of what he taught us about how we should use our hearts to guide our lives and treat other people. An early inkling of my Jewish heritage was your characterization of Jesus as a teacher and prophet. Both of you were always for the underdog; not tolerating racism, bigotry or exclusivity.

When Susie and I found your original marriage certificate that was signed by a Rabbi, it was ever-clear that you both were Jewish; in fact, I talked to a Rabbi in West Hartford Connecticut who

confirmed this as well, along with the little bit of information that I had about you. He very gently asked me what I wanted to do with the information and I said "nothing." I thought that just knowing would be enough.

Well, it wasn't enough. I needed to know more and fill in the gaps and empty spaces about our family. So I started doing research a few years ago. I found mom's record of her voyage to the U.S. from Cherbourg, France. I also found out that she came here with her stepmother, Irma Servos. Mom, you had told me that your father was in the French underground and disappeared when you were about 13 years old - what I didn't know until I started researching through the U.S. Holocaust Memorial Museum Washington, D.C., that he was murdered by the Nazis in 1942. When I found out, it felt like he had died at that moment; the grief was so intense that I couldn't even take it in. Mom, you had also told me that your stepmother was abusive to you. So awful to even think about how painful that must have been for you to find out years later that she was not your birth mother. I know now that your birth mother's name was Ellen Schwarz - I wish I had more information about her but it's difficult to communicate with the officials in Germany, which is how I found that information.

Dad - I had no idea that so many in your family went to Auschwitz. I learned that your sister Blanche survived four different concentration camps after losing her husband to the murderous Nazis. How wonderful that you helped her get to the U.S. after the war. And how wonderful that she spent her life married to her second husband Tony, whose daughter I found and met just last year through my research. She had nothing but wonderful things to say about Blanche, who died in 2005. And your parents, Julia and Jakob Adler, appear on a list of deportees who were also murdered. I went to Slovakia just last year, to the town of Topoľčany where you were raised and was horrified to see the devastation that still exists from the Nazi and Communist occupations.

In the town offices, I was assisted by two women and through a translator, they told me about the town of Žilina, also in Slovakia, the last known location I was able to find for your parents. What I found out was that Žilina was a holding station for Jews to be *taken and murdered. These two women were so kind in having to relate this devastating news to me. I felt such pain and emptiness thinking of all you had told me about your happy childhood living in this small town with your sisters and brother and parents. I still wonder how you were able to get out of Czechoslovakia in 1939 when you finished medical school; and it is still remarkable to me that you joined the British Army and came to the U.S. and went through exams, citizenship processes and more to be able to practice medicine in this country. And to get married again in the Presbyterian Church when I was five years old and Susie was eight; and raise us in your own interpretation of Christian tradition by living the values that Jesus taught. I can't imagine what it would be like to decide to leave your faith out of fear and persecution and adopt a completely new one.*

I'll always wonder how the two of you were able to raise me and Susie in the most loving and protective way after what you and your families experienced. What a joy to be your daughter. I still miss you. I wish you could see Bonnie and her wonderful husband and my three beautiful grandchildren. And Susie's two grandbabies, two beautiful little boys. And you would love my husband.

I'll write more soon. Love and peace to you both.

"HIDING IN PLAIN SIGHT" is Orlene Allen Gallops' account of discovering her Jewish Heritage, her research and personal journey as she uncovered her family's unspeakable loss and desire to leave the past behind.

Orlene's career spans decades in the Employee Assistance (EAP) field, providing consultation and crisis support to major financial services and health care organizations and their employees. After she retired in 2012, she formed Gallops Consulting, where she provides consulting, program evaluation, training, and education for area and global businesses. She holds an M.A. in Counseling from the University of St. Joseph's in West Hartford, Connecticut and a B.A. in Sociology from Queens College of the City University of New York.

Orlene lives in Old Saybrook, Connecticut with her husband John.